THE COST OF COLORS:
A Coach's Story

THE COST OF COLORS:
A Coach's Story

A Memoir

Ronnie Mitchem

XULON PRESS

Xulon Press Elite
2301 Lucien Way #415
Maitland, FL 32751
407.339.4217
www.xulonpress.com

First Edition 2019

ISBN-13: 978-1-54566-400-1
        978-1-54566-401-8
eBook ISBN-13: 978-1-54566-402-5

FOR MY WIFE, STACEY
Who stands with me always.

FOR OUR CHILDREN: KERSTIN, LYNZIE, AND CHASE
You are my heart and soul.

FOR MY HEROES
*My Momma, Melissa Brown Winkler, and my sister,
Rhonda Halstead.*

FOR MY CHURCH, VICTORY & PRAISE WORSHIP CENTER
Your support and encouragement are deeply appreciated.

FOR MY FOOTBALL PROGRAM, THE V&P SHARKS
*Your hard work and dedication showed the world what
"More than just football" meant.*

and

FOR ALL US VETERANS
Thank you for your service.

Author's Note

This is a memoir, and it presents my recollections of experiences over time. My memories are not perfect, but I am sharing them to the best of my knowledge. Unless otherwise attributed, the beliefs and opinions expressed in this memoir are solely mine. Some names and characteristics have been changed to protect anonymity, some events have been compressed, and some dialogue has been recreated.

THE COST OF COLORS:
A Coach's Story

CONTENTS

_____

FOREWORD

⸻

P eople ask me if I regret what happened that night in
Tomball, Texas. My answer is no, not one single bit.

Coach Ronnie Mitchem and I had discussed with our
players on numerous occasions that despite the NFL allowing
its teams to protest by kneeling during the national anthem,
our high school football team, the Victory & Praise Sharks,
would not under any circumstances follow suit. Every time
we discussed this with the team—*every time*—the consequences were conveyed very clearly: You kneel; you're done.
No questions asked.

And yet, for several reasons, which Coach Mitchem
reveals in this book, two of our players still decided to protest as our national anthem played. It was heartbreaking to
watch boys so young disregard and disrespect the values this
country has fought for her entire life.

Coach Mitchem, true to his word, immediately and
respectfully removed the boys from the team, and, in doing
so, unleashed a firestorm of criticism lit by the mainstream
media. The days, weeks, and months that followed were

by far the hardest times we had seen as the Sharks family. "Feedback" that Ronnie received from some very vile people was tough for me, as his friend, to see and hear, as was the physical and emotional stress he and his family endured. And yet not one single time did Coach second-guess or regret his decision.

To me, Coach Mitchem is a true example of an American patriot. He fought for our country in a way that no one in the football community ever has. From peewee leagues to the NFL, no one has stood up for all those who laid down their lives for our freedom. None of them said, "This is wrong, and we're going to do something about it." None of them said, "If you kneel, you're fired." But my best friend did.

The man who coached a small six-man high school football team in Crosby, Texas, stood up to the world, to the protesters, to the hate-mongers, to the race baiters, and to the very people who are responsible for the situation that America is in today and said, "No." No, we will not kneel. No, we will not disrespect all those who have served. No, we will not submit to your hate. And no, we will not falter. This is what true patriotism is. This is what America is. And this is why the Victory & Praise Sharks football team from Crosby, Texas, will always be remembered.

Brad Wilson
Assistant Football Coach
V&P Sharks

PREFACE

On US military installations around the world, morning and evening colors—the ceremonial raising and lowering of the flag—is as routine as breathing, and for the men and women serving in uniform, just as needful. Those who wear the cloth of our nation have always been closest to the flag; it's real to them and much more than a symbol. They've held it in their hands—unfolding it in the morning to raise above themselves, and folding it again, with great respect and gratitude, as the sun sets on the fallen. I pray that we never forget the love, devotion, and sacrifice of our sailors, Marines, airmen, and soldiers who keep America's colors alive at all cost because preserving freedom costs all.

We live in a time when our country is sorely divided; some even describe it as another civil war. No formal declaration of war has been made, but battles are taking place, and people are choosing which side of politics to defend—the right or the left. Every day in the news we hear of conservative casualties—coaches, teachers, and students whose jobs and reputations are critically injured because they stood for American and Christian values.

I know what I'm talking about because it happened to me. I stood up for the national anthem and the flag when both were protested at a high-school level football game. As a former Marine, I refused to let the flag be dishonored and disrespected by two teenage players on the team that I coached. But when I exercised my right to cut them from my football program, I found myself in a fierce fight for my integrity, reputation, and even my life.

There is nothing civil about this war, and it looks to last for some time. Two versions of America are struggling to exist: one is the country I know and love—the one that holds "these truths to be self-evident, that all men are created equal, that they are endowed by their Creator with certain unalienable rights, that among these are life, liberty, and the pursuit of happiness," as stated in the Declaration of Independence. The other is working to change the truth of God into a lie, and worship and serve the creature more than the Creator (Rom. 1:25).

When wars break out, the call to serve follows. To me, other than the Word of God, nothing is more inspiring than learning about the men and women who answer that call. One of my favorite true stories is about Sgt. William H. Carney, the first black recipient of the Medal of Honor. He was born into slavery, but he and his family were later granted freedom. It seems that he wanted to be a minister of the gospel, perhaps because he knew that the only cure for man's oppression of man is the blood of Jesus Christ. But when the Civil War started, Carney said, "I could best serve my God serving my country and my oppressed brothers."[1]

In 1863, his regiment led the charge on Fort Wagner.[2] Back then, each unit was assigned a "color bearer" — an unarmed soldier who carried the flag. In the chaos of the fight, soldiers would look for the flag to regain formation and hold the line. The enemy also looked for the flag. They saw it as an easy target, and most color bearers were critically injured or killed. When one fell, another soldier was quick to take up the flag and move forward.[3] That's what earned Carney the Medal of Honor.

An 1864 issue of *The United States Service Magazine* reported his action this way: "As our forces retire, Sergeant Carney, who has kept the colors of his regiment flying upon the parapet of Wagner during the entire conflict, is seen creeping along on one knee, still holding up the flag, and only yielding its sacred trust upon finding an officer of his regiment. As he enters the field-hospital, where his wounded comrades are being brought in, they cheer him and the colors. Though nearly exhausted with the loss of blood, he says, 'Boys, the old flag never touched the ground.'"[4]

Carney was given our nation's highest honor not for saving the lives of other men, but for protecting the American flag. How is it that what our country honored then is so dishonored now?

This book is my humble attempt at a call for more color bearers in this ongoing battle of respect for our national anthem and our flag. May we never let either touch the ground.

Semper Fi.

INTRODUCTION

"You know this has gone national, don't you?"

I leaned around the cameraman who had just clipped a mic to my shirt, so I could see the reporter talking to me. He was looking down at his iPad, scrolling.

"National?" I asked.

"Yes, and really beyond that. BBC, ESPN, CNN, MSNBC, Reuters — you name it. They all have this story."

I was stunned. I coached a six-man football team in a Texas town of less than 3,000 people. At our last game, during the national anthem, two of my players decided to protest after I'd told them not to. So I did what I'd told the whole team I'd do if that happened: I kicked them off. Now I was news.

Before our TV interview started, I asked the reporter, "Am I the only coach in America to do what I did?"

"Yes, at least as far as we know at this time. All set?"

I went into that first interview still shell-shocked that this story had garnered so much media attention. But here I was, in front of a television camera, to give my side of it. I'd never done such an interview. Now, several were lined up for the day.

My emotions spun in every direction. How had all of this happened? Just the day before I'd been preparing the team to play the fourth game of our 2017 football season. Now I was a coach (and a pastor) in the national spotlight, doing the first of several interviews, and the questions, I learned, came fast and pointed.

"Have you been boycotting the NFL?"

"Yes, I have been and will continue to boycott the NFL."

"Did what the president say about it have any effect on you and your decision?"

"No, what President Trump said had no bearing on my thoughts about the kneeling."

"Did you vote for Trump?"

"I did vote for President Trump, but his opinion on this did not make me feel the way I do about the kneeling. Even if the president or anybody else thought it was okay, I do not."

As the interview progressed, the reporter fired off questions flavored with accusation, as if I had done something wrong, and he was trying to make me admit guilt. I kept wondering what it was that he wanted from me.

I repeated for him the bottom line: "I have team rules. Those rules were broken by two players who knew the rules and the consequences for breaking those rules."

That first interview was a blur, and I did my best to get through it. All I could think about was how much I wanted it to end so I could go and find a place to be alone with God and pray.

My daughter and son-in-law had come to the church to lend me support during the media interviews and to serve as witnesses to what I actually said during each one. After the news crews left, the three of us talked about how it all went.

"Did it look okay to you guys?" I asked.

"It got better as you went along," my daughter said. "At first, when the reporter told you the story had gone national, it looked like someone had slapped you."

CHAPTER 1

WEATHER WARNINGS

———⟶

It was the summer of 2017, and we were all excited about the upcoming football season.

We had a right to be; we were coming off of an 8–2 record that included a win over our crosstown rival, the Fort Bend Chargers, with a 92–67 victory. Our two losses that season were to NYOS (Not Your Ordinary School) Charter of Austin—a thriller that led to overtime—and to Bastrop (we lost in the first round of the playoffs). Bastrop ended up playing for the state title.

That year, everything pointed to our team, the Victory & Praise Sharks, as serious contenders for the 2017 Texas Association of Independent Athletic Organizations (TAIAO) Division II state title.

In fact, a coach who had won a TAIAO Division I state championship told me, "There is no doubt about it, buddy; you'll win state Division II, and I can't wait to watch y'all win it. I'm gonna be there."

I drove from Houston to Austin with Coach Larry Pavlik to attend the annual TAIAO conference. After losing to his team for the past four years, I was looking forward to him buying me a victory steak dinner instead of the other way around.

On the drive, we talked a little bit about the protests being made by NFL players who refused to stand during the national anthem before their televised games started. For the past year or so, these professional players were choosing to sit or kneel as America's song played in protest against racial and social injustice.

The first time I saw it happen, my heart sank.

Larry and I both coached six-man football teams in a program created for homeschool, charter, and private school students whose schools didn't offer football. Our teams were small, but these protests — covered heavily by the mainstream media — were edging closer to places like Sugar Land and Crosby where our boys played.

"Think it'll come up at the conference?" Larry asked.

"I think it should," I said. "We started these football programs on our own dime, and my boys know how I feel about this. They know that when the anthem plays, you show respect and stand."

Unfortunately, not everybody at the conference felt the same way I did. One coach announced that for his games, he would ask the coach of the visiting team if he thought any of those players would kneel during the national anthem. "If so, we'll just skip the playing of the anthem," he said.

Larry asked TAIAO president Wayne Alldredge, "So, are you saying that we should all do this as a league, or are you just letting us know that this was one coach's way of handling this kneeling issue inside his own program?"

When other coaches raised similar questions, Alldredge made it clear this was not league policy, and that each coach should handle it the way he felt was best for his team.

As a former US Marine, I knew that I would always play the national anthem at my games regardless of who did or didn't like it. In my opinion, this kneeling had become a hot media topic, which had been manipulated into a race issue. It had nothing to do with race and everything to do with respect (and disrespect). The way I saw it, the act of kneeling was the act of a traitor — a Benedict Arnold. To turn it into a race issue was absurd. Men and women of all colors have fought and died for American freedoms, and to see people who enjoy those freedoms kneel was the same for me as watching someone spit on the graves of those who gave the fullest measure for this great country.

America may not be perfect, but no country is. Yet despite all of her faults, there is none better than these United States, and anyone who doesn't think so should feel free to leave. But to spread around the world a false idea and image of racism in our country is not fair or just.

Just look how far America has come. In 2008, the first black man was elected president of the United States, and he won a second term in 2012. Several major cities in this nation are led by black mayors. Likewise, we have black police chiefs in large cities, including Chicago, where, in my opinion, much of the debate on social injustice originated.

I have a real hard time believing that a black police chief and other black officers would go along with the negative narrative claiming that police officers are targeting and killing black people. Sorry, this is fake news, and I'm not buying it. I believe many of these shooting incidents hinge on a respect issue. I also think that when a person resists arrest, he only causes himself problems. If a person refuses to show respect to law enforcement, then he shouldn't expect to receive respect in return.

Children today are being taught at home, in school, and on the streets to disrespect and hate America, and I find that troubling. So, when this whole kneeling thing started, I had no doubt as to how I would handle it regarding my team. At practices, I talked about it with my players more than once.

"For every one of our games," I said, "the national anthem will play, and out of respect for our country and for our flag, you will stand. Sitting or kneeling at any time during the anthem will not be tolerated. If it happens, you will be off this team. Everybody got that?"

All the boys shouted back, "Yes, sir!"

On the drive back to Houston, Larry and I discussed what we'd been told at the conference. For our games, we both decided that the national anthem would play, and our boys would stand.

Larry has high respect for veterans and a great love for his country. In fact, several men in his family served in the military, including his son.

He and I got along every day of the year, except for about four hours on the day our teams played against each other.

Even then, win or lose, we still shook hands. The only time our five-year friendship was tested was on that drive home from the conference, when Larry bought us some cheap barbecue instead of the steak dinner he owed me.

Larry and I met in 2012 when we both started football programs for boys in our area, who wanted to play football but had no program at the schools they attended. We also wanted to help these young men learn discipline and respect, and show them that hard work really does pay off.

More important, we wanted to help them put Jesus Christ first in their lives. This was a lesson I'd learned when I left public school in the seventh grade and enrolled at Bell Road Christian School. I had a coach who put God first, and he showed me how to live for Christ on and off the field.

So I know firsthand how sports can be used as a powerful tool for the gospel when dealing with young people and their Christianity. The football field is a great place to teach boys life lessons about being a man—lessons that also work well toward being good husbands and fathers.

At the beginning of each new season, I huddle the boys up and give them my "talk":

> Welcome to the Shark family, and we are a family. Each day, when you show up for practice, you will shake each coach's hand and tell him hello. The way to shake a man's hand is to look him square in the eye and give his hand a firm shake. At the end of each practice, you will shake each coach's hand and tell him thank

5

you. This is done so that we all leave on good terms. We are here to work hard and become the best team we can be, and that means we will sometimes have to push you.

While wearing your Shark uniform, win or lose, you will show class, you will show Christ, and you will show sportsmanship—always. We will not curse you, and you will not curse us. You will not curse during games. Respect one another and respect your opponents. No trash talking will be allowed. Let your playing do your talking.

Play between the whistles fast and hard, blocking and tackling, because the only bad tackle is the one you don't make; the only bad block is the one you don't make. Play like a team. Know your assignment and do it—every single play. If you miss a block or a tackle, shake it off and determine it will be the only one missed this game.

We want you to give your best every play. At practice, you need to push yourself on the drills and sprints to be in better shape than your opponent. Embrace the heat during practice and know that it will help you get in better shape when you get under the lights on Friday night. If you practice hard during the week, your easiest day will be Friday night. Football is a great way to prepare you to be a man because when you don't feel like practicing or running another play, you have to suck it up and be a man—be a Shark.

Play like every play is the last one. Don't waste one snap—make them all count. Don't worry about the other team. Don't worry about the scoreboard. Worry about doing your job every play. If everybody does his job to the best of his ability, then we will be unbeatable, and you will understand why the slogan of the V&P Sharks is, "It's more than just football."

The fall of 2017 was no different. We started practice in the hot August sun and worked hard to accomplish something special. At the end of our fall practice, we participated in a four-team scrimmage at a large private school in downtown Houston, just blocks from the NRG Stadium where the Houston Texans play. We did great in the scrimmage, and it looked as if our spring training and fall practice had served us well because every team in that stadium played in a higher division than we did.

We left that field very excited about our team. The only thing I worried about was our senior wide receiver, Yale Jay, who had suffered a knee injury that ended his season. This left a big void in our game plan. Somebody would have to step up and take Yale's place.

As we left the field that day, we noticed the first storm clouds of Hurricane Harvey shadowing the Houston skyline. We were glad we had gotten in our scrimmage game before the storm hit. Weather warnings had called for heavy rains and flooding in our area—not unusual for southeast Texas—but we had no idea of what Harvey would do to Houston.

The next day, August 25, 2017, Harvey made landfall. Heavy rains—two feet in the first 24 hours[1]—flooded the Houston area. Since water had covered most cars, boats were used to travel up and down residential streets to rescue people who were trapped in their homes. Submerged neighborhoods looked like lakes with a rooftop here and there coming up for air. Rescue boats manned by law enforcement and volunteers worked around the clock to get those who were stranded to dry ground. The devastation that happened to the fourth largest city in America was unbelievable, and no one could stop it.

Floodwater is a damaging force, especially to homes. It rushes into rooms too quickly to save anything, so furniture, family photos, and keepsakes all fall victim. As a result of this storm, more than thirty-nine thousand people were forced out of their homes and into shelters and hotels.[2]

Since our house is elevated, my family and I were surrounded by water, but it didn't get inside our home, which happens to sit next door to the church I pastor. From our house, we watched as the water inched closer and closer to the church. I prayed and asked God to please stop the rain, but the rain kept coming.

A couple in our church, Glen and Vickey Fulcher, weren't as fortunate as we were. The storm claimed their home, and they needed a place to stay. We invited them and their family to move in with us. Despite our concerns that the church might still flood, we went ahead and opened its doors to those desperate for a place to stay.

It rained so hard that our dog, Mikee, made his way into our boat and wouldn't leave it, as if he knew the danger we faced. Our associate pastor, Stan Oliver—one of my dearest friends—called me to say that his house was about to go under. Stan lived on the bank of the San Jacinto River, which flows into the Lake Houston reservoir. Due to the heavy rainfall, they had to open the gates of the dam upstream to keep it from breaking or being compromised. Normally, homeowners there didn't worry about flooding since they lived between two dams, but this was no normal rainstorm.

Glen and I tried to reach Stan's house to see if we could help. We were able to drive some of the way, but the road we needed was blocked by high water. I tried to call him but no luck. The last time I had talked to Stan, he mentioned that his boat was tied up nearby, just in case he needed it.

I felt helpless. All I could do was pray that God would keep him safe, and He did. Unfortunately, Stan's house did flood, along with his daughter's home, but at least they made it out alive. Sadly, eighty-eight people did not.[3] They lost their lives in that hurricane, a storm that continued to dump rain in Louisiana, Mississippi, and all the way up to Kentucky.[4]

When the last gallon of rain fell—and Harvey dropped thirty-three trillion[5]—the water started to recede. I contacted all of our church members and my football players to make sure that everyone was safe and to ask if they needed any help. Everyone, thank God, was fine. I ventured away from the house and church to see the devastation. I was shocked. As far as cost in damages, only Katrina beat out Harvey.[6]

As they were able, those displaced left the temporary shelters and returned to their homes to see what was left. The stories of loss were heartbreaking to hear, but no one took the time to feel sorry for themselves. The people in and around Houston went to work. They tore out carpets, hauled wet furniture to the curb, and ripped away mildewed sheetrock. It was a sight to see—neighbors helping neighbors, and complete strangers showing up to work.

Several of my football players volunteered with the cleanup efforts. Our church folks made sandwiches and cold drinks for the workers. I cherish that image of all those brothers and sisters in the Lord—white, black, and Hispanic—all working together in our fellowship hall and doing what they could to help. I will never forget the pride I felt seeing the best of people during one of the nation's worst natural disasters.

Nobody cared about skin color or whether someone was rich or poor. People just wanted to help one another. Up to that point, I had never been crazy about living in the Houston area. I only moved there because I felt that the Lord led me there. But in the aftermath of Harvey and seeing that sort of teamwork among neighbors and strangers alike, for the first time, I felt proud of the city I now call home.

My family, the church, and everyone we knew in the Houston area was thankful that the hurricane had finally passed. We were ready to get back to our lives, at least as best we could. For me, that meant pastoring the church and coaching football.

But another storm was brewing — one that would change my life forever. Yes, sir, heading my way were winds and rain strong enough to drown out a man's name, his faith, and his voice. Only this time there would be no warning.

CHAPTER 2

ON THE SIDELINES

O ur first two football games of the 2017 season were canceled due to the hurricane. This may not seem like a big deal in other places, but if you know anything about Texas, then you know that folks here are crazy about high school football, and a good old-fashioned football game is just what our community needed.

So we quickly put together a game between our team and High Island ISD (Independent School District). Not only did the event help people regain a sense of normalcy following the hurricane, but it also served as a way to help us collect some desperately needed supplies to help flood victims in Houston.

The boys were used to playing in the heat and humidity, which is normal that time of year, but after all that rain, the air was extra thick and steamy. And the time off from Harvey hadn't helped our team's conditioning. Even so, the Cardinals and the Sharks did not disappoint the fans (or the coaches). They battled through a hard-fought game, scoring a lot of points. In the end, we won, 61–57, but not without injuries.

We left that field beat up with little time to recover before playing a tough team the following week — Annapolis Christian in Corpus Christi.

The day before we left for Corpus, I found out that two of our thirteen players — Larry McCullough and Cedric "CJ" Ingram-Lewis — would not be making the trip. With so little notice, I had no time to prepare or change our game plan. I thought we'd be okay with just eleven boys, but I was wrong; we lost. Even so, the boys fought hard — injuries and all. They never gave up.

Our next game was against the defending state champs of our league, THESA. They had twenty-eight players and played in Division I. We played in the smaller Division II, and we would need all hands on deck if we were to have any chance against them.

The next week, we headed to Fort Worth for the game. I always drove our church van, pulling a trailer loaded with our equipment, and I encouraged the players to ride to the game together with me. After the game, most of the boys rode home with their parents.

Traffic was awful on the way to Fort Worth, but the boys didn't notice. As usual, they were busy talking, joking, or listening to music. You really get to know your players when you're locked in a van with them for hours at a time. It can be quite entertaining.

During one of our stops, I was pumping gas and noticed that Larry was still inside the van. As soon as we'd stopped, the other boys jumped out and headed into the gas mart to buy drinks and snacks, but Larry stayed behind just like he had for every other stop.

When I saw that none of the other boys were around, I asked Larry, "Do you need some money?"

"No, sir," he said. "I'm not hungry."

When I finished at the gas pump, I checked with him one more time. "Sure I can't get you a Gatorade, Larry?"

"No, sir. I'm good."

We finally made it to our hotel in Fort Worth. I was in the lobby making sure that all the boys were getting checked into their rooms when I noticed CJ at the front desk. He was paying cash for his room, and the clerk said the hotel policy was a $50 deposit on cash transactions. CJ didn't have it with him, so I put up the $50.

My wife, Stacey, and I had done this many times for kids. We knew that without our help, they simply would not get to play ball.

I remember one kid who played on our team, and my wife and I noticed that he never had any money to buy meals on our road trips. So, before every game, when nobody was around, we would hand him $20. We also decided not to charge him the usual athletic fees for our football program because we knew he didn't have the money, but he wanted to play. We also knew that this young man didn't live with his parents. I had hoped that these kindnesses would minister to him, but I guess I failed because when he quit the team mid-season, he decided to keep all of my football equipment, including the uniform.

Over the years, I have worked with families to find a way to keep their kids playing football. My wife and I realized that a lot of people were struggling financially, especially after the hurricane.

I only mention this because I want people to know how much I cared about each one of my players. Whenever I gave a kid food or hotel money, I never expected it back. But uniforms and equipment are very expensive to replace. Unlike public schools, my football program received no funding from the state or the government, so a good portion of the costs often came out of my own pocket. And we did get some help from our football and church families — a parent might slip me some gas money to fill up the church van or a gift card for a restaurant, and every so often we'd have a fundraiser at the church, all of which helped to offset some of the team's travel expenses.

We did what it took to make it work because to me, our football program was a ministry, and I treated it no differently than I did my church.

Ever since we started Victory & Praise Worship Center, we have always tried to help people in need. I have given to people even when I wasn't sure how we would pay our own bills, but God has always made a way for us. Money cannot stand in the way of ministry and the preaching of the gospel of Jesus Christ. Faith is the most important part, and I know that when you do God's work, He will provide.

In Fort Worth, when I got into my own hotel room, I checked my emails before meeting with the team, and

I was more than surprised to see one from the Houston Texans. It read:

> Congratulations! Because of your impact, you have been selected as our Houston Texans Coach of the Week award recipient for week four! You will receive a donation from the Houston Texans Foundation and Houston Methodist for $2,500 for your football program! As well as a signed certificate from Houston Texans Head Coach Bill O'Brien! We would love to recognize you during one of your practices! Please let me know which day during the week of Oct. 2 that would work best for your program. We look forward to hearing from you soon!
>
> —The Houston Texans

The note went on to say that the reason I had being selected was because my players and their parents had nominated me.

I was shocked and somewhat afraid that it wasn't real, so I didn't say anything about it except to my wife and son. Until then, I hadn't received such an honor from my players or their parents. My program has always been about the players, not me. But it was nice to think that after six years of coaching, I was going to be recognized, and to top it off, my program would receive $2,500, which we desperately needed to pay for new uniforms.

That night we went on to play a great game against THESA; we scored first. At half-time, we were only down by 10 points, which wasn't bad for a 45-point underdog. Going into the fourth quarter, we still only trailed by 10 points. Those THESA boys were not happy about it, and they got a little extra fired up, which didn't sit well with one of our team parents. CJ's mom and Larry's aunt, Rhonda Brady, was yelling back at the THESA players. Afterward, my assistant coach, Brad Wilson said, "She acted up to the point that Larry had to calm her down and keep her from making a fool of herself."

To make matters worse, the referees weren't the best we'd seen. Coach Wilson and I felt THESA was getting a lot of play after the whistle was blown. When I heard a few of their players getting a little mouthy, to be honest, I got frustrated too and said some negative things about them and their program. The chain crew — mostly parents of players from the other team — heard what I said. I knew it was wrong as soon as I said it, and I did my best to make it right with a text to THESA's athletic director:

> Coach, I hope you will share this with your team coaches and fans:
>
> I would like to apologize for my behavior and that of our fans while playing you last Friday night. I said some things on the sideline about your coaching staff and team that I should not have said. I want to apologize to your people

who worked the chains. I have no excuse for what I did other than it was a rough day even before we got to your field. I had other issues with parents that night from my team, which caused me to be very negative toward anybody and everybody. Just like your coach has worked to build a Christian-based football program, I have done the same with our program. I started V&P Sharks six years ago and have tried to teach our young men to play with class and character, win or lose. My team will be a better team for playing an outstanding football team like yours, and we would like to keep a good relationship with the THESA football family. Hoping THESA will win another state title in 2017.

—Coach Ronnie Mitchem, V&P
Sharks Football

If I didn't want my players talking trash, I had to set the example. The assistant coaches and I teach them to do their talking between the whistles by hitting hard and then getting up and returning to huddle. Since that THESA game, I got to know both the head coach and the athletic director, and found them to be strong Christian men.

Honestly, the boys on the other team acted mildly compared to some other teams we've played. I later realized that I had gotten upset mainly because I wanted to beat that team, and they couldn't believe that they were struggling so hard with this little team from Crosby.

After that game, we met in the middle of the field and had prayer together. Then I gathered my team on our sideline and began our after-game talk. I was still talking when CJ walked off, toward the other sideline.

"What's going on?" I asked.

One of the guys spoke up. "CJ's mom is on the other side hollering at their team's fans and coaches."

Rhonda had marched across the football field, found the THESA coach and, judging from her body language, was extremely angry with him. It got to a point where Coach Wilson and Coach Sammon trotted over to try to help diffuse what was quickly becoming a heated exchange, but when Rhonda saw our coaches approaching, she backed off. Later that night, Coach Wilson explained how Rhonda was very upset with me for not forfeiting the game when the "dirty play" was going on, and she accused me of not caring about her boys.

I finished my after-game talk with the rest of the team, and someone mentioned that Rhonda was mad at me, so when I saw her walking down the sideline, I called out to her. I made my way over to her and asked why she was upset.

"You should have forfeited the game," she said.

"Why?"

"It's all fun and games until the two black boys go to jail."

I was completely shocked by what she said. I honestly had no idea where such a statement came from.

The other team's players may have gotten a little feisty, but that's football. During the game, I never saw anything racist happen. Both teams had white, black, and Hispanic players. The officials may not have been the best, but three of them were black, and the head official was Hispanic.

Rhonda had never been very friendly to me, but she had never made a scene like this before.

I asked Stacey if she knew why Rhonda had acted the way she did.

"No, I don't," she said. "Before the game, I went over and greeted her and the other parents.

"And how was Rhonda?"

"Rhonda was her usual self," which I knew meant unfriendly.

For Rhonda, that was nothing out of the ordinary. As far as I knew, she had never tried to socialize with the other football parents. I can remember only twice that she was ever somewhat nice to me, and even then she was standoffish.

Another one of our team moms, Valerie Keene, told me how all the Shark parents were upset that night. She was especially concerned because one of her sons got an injury in that game that kept him out for a couple of weeks.

Valerie later told me, "We were all highly irritated and flat out mad at the other team's coaches and the refs for such a dirty game, but we all stayed on our side of the field and kept our comments among ourselves because that's how you expect your players and their parents to act—with respect. But Rhonda did what she wanted to do and stormed across the field and yelled at the other team's coaches and the refs."

21

Then Valerie reminded me, "And you know as well as I do that this wasn't the first confrontation Larry and CJ's family has had with the refs."

After my sideline conversation with Rhonda, I didn't see her, CJ, or Larry again that night or the next day when we left to head back home to Crosby. On the drive back, and for a few days afterward, I kept thinking about what she had said and why.

As a pastor, I've learned how to read people, and I understand that everybody is different. Some people are friendly, some are not, and some are shy, which can be misinterpreted as unfriendliness. Others take a little time to warm up to folks they don't know. Stan claims that I've never met a stranger and that I can talk to anyone. I'm not sure about that, but I do try to treat everyone with respect, which is why the conversation with Rhonda had me so troubled.

A few days later, we had moved on from our trip to Fort Worth and found ourselves getting ready to play a team we had never faced before—Providence Classical—located about an hour from us. After traveling to Corpus Christi and Fort Worth, it was great to have a game closer to home.

We would have a normal week with practices on Monday and Tuesday in pads. Because we are a Christian football team, and I preach at church on Wednesdays, we normally show game film that day, or give the boys a day off. On Thursdays, we have a walk through and go over special teams in shorts and helmets.

This week would be no different, or so I thought.

CHAPTER 3

KAEPERNICK

"It's all fun and games until the two black boys go to jail." Rhonda's racially charged words following the THESA game still didn't make any sense to me. In my mind, what she said didn't connect. Was she referring to what really happened at our local game, or to the bigger football issue of the day—the ongoing protests against social injustice by NFL players?

For more than a year, certain NFL players had chosen to follow Colin Kaepernick's lead, either by sitting or kneeling during the national anthem at their televised football games.[1] Although he had done it for every 2016 preseason game, no one really noticed until August 26, when Niners Nation beat writer Jennifer Lee Chan tweeted a photo of Kaepernick sitting during the anthem before a game against the Green Bay Packers.[2]

In the predawn hours of August 27, *ProFootballTalk's* Mike Florio posted a story with a statement by the San Francisco 49ers that ended with, "we recognize the right of an individual to choose to participate, or not, in celebration of the national anthem."[3]

By this time, Chan's photo had circled the social media circuit, and she was bombarded with media requests for her photo from Fox News, the Associated Press, ABC, *Sports Illustrated*, CBS, and others.

The media wanted the story behind this image, and Kaepernick, it seemed, wanted to tell it.

On August 28, he met with reporters, and, in an unusually calm and almost sympathetic exchange between the media and Kaepernick, he answered thirty inquiries as to why he sat down during the national anthem.[4] I've seen fewer questions asked during a Barbara Walters special.

One reporter threw somewhat of a hardball and asked Kaepernick if he was concerned that his action might be viewed as a "blanket indictment" of law enforcement. The question seemed to irritate Kaepernick, and his answer irritated me, especially the part where he compared the training and education of police officers who risk their lives every day for our protection to that of hairdressers.[5] (To be fair, I wanted to reprint Kaepernick's word-for-word answers from this "press conference" here, but I was told that *if* I received permission to print a portion of this transcript in my book, the cost of its use started at $4,500 per video minute, and this interview was more than eighteen minutes long. Nothing about the free press, I've learned, is free.)

Other reporters who disagreed with Kaepernick started digging around the root reasons for his protesting.

In an article titled, "Colin Kaepernick Making a Misguided Stand," David Whitley of the *Orlando Sentinel* asked, "Do we still have the right to be insulted when people dishonor the flag?"[6]

He went on to point out the same quote that Florio mentioned in his breaking story — Kaepernick's re-tweet from August 25, which showed images of the Confederate and American flags with the caption, "The fact that you really believe that there is difference in these flags means that your [sic] ignoring history."[7]

Also in this last week of August, Kaepernick showed up for a postgame news conference wearing a T-shirt with six black-and-white images of communist dictator Fidel Castro with Malcom X under a caption that read, "Like Minds Think Alike."[8]

Up to this point, I had viewed Kaepernick's national anthem sit-out as something a spoiled child would do — pout. He wasn't getting his way on the field, so he used football to turn national attention onto himself, as if playing quarterback for the NFL wasn't a big enough spotlight.

But when I saw Kaepernick on the news in that Castro shirt, I couldn't wrap my head around why anyone would endorse such imagery by modeling it, especially at a press conference.

When I think of Fidel Castro, I think of Florida 1980 — the year of the Mariel Boatlift. Castro had announced that if any Cubans wanted to immigrate to the United States, they could, and a hundred and twenty-five thousand people took him up on his offer. I was only fourteen at the time, but even I realized that things must have been pretty bad in Cuba for so many people to leave everything behind and risk a ninety-mile boat trip across the Straits of Florida, some clutching for life to their homemade rafts and inner tubes.[9]

So for someone who claimed to "stand" for social justice while wearing a Castro shirt in front of the press sent, in my opinion, a very mixed message.

Soon after that, *The Los Angeles Times* ran a photo of Kaepernick wearing socks with images of pigs dressed like police officers taken during an August 10 training camp.[10]

In an Instagram post to his 3.2 million followers, Kaepernick responded to the situation: "I wore these socks, in the past, because the rogue cops that are allowed to hold positions in police departments, not only put the community in danger, but also put the cops that have the right intentions in danger by creating an environment of tension and mistrust."[11]

Under public pressure for response, the NFL chimed in on Kaepernick's kneeling saying, "Players are encouraged but not required to stand during the playing of the national anthem."[12] The organization made it clear that such protesting would be tolerated, and less than a week later, in a show of support for Kaepernick, Seattle Seahawks cornerback Jeremy Lane sat during the anthem in a preseason game against the Oakland Raiders. Lane told ESPN, "I just like what he's doing, and I'm standing behind him. It's something I plan on keep on doing, until I feel like justice is being served."[13]

By September players from the Kansas City Chiefs, the Miami Dolphins, the Denver Broncos, and the New England Patriots had joined the protest by kneeling, holding up their right arms, or raising a black-gloved fist during their televised games as the national anthem played.[14]

Despite public backlash, NFL Commissioner Roger Goodell, in my opinion, refused to take a definitive stand on the issue. He told the Associated Press, "I support our players when they want to see change in society, and we don't live in a perfect society. On the other hand, we believe very strongly in patriotism in the NFL. I personally believe very strongly in that."[15]

With two-thirds of the NFL players being black,[16] Goodell was giving diplomacy his best shot, but those offended by the protests expected more from the nearly 100-year-old National Football League, an organization skilled at dealing with controversy and scandal.

Kneeling during the anthem continued, and strong reactions—both for and against—rippled across the political landscape and throughout professional sports.

With the 2016 presidential campaign in full swing, Republican presidential nominee Donald Trump was asked about Kaepernick's ongoing protest. He told *The Dori Monson Show*, "I have followed it, and I think it's personally not a good thing. I think it's a terrible thing, and you know, maybe he should find a country that works better for him. Let him try; it's not gonna happen."[17]

Trump's opponent, Hillary Clinton, was too busy fighting off past scandals and rumors of poor health to comment

THE COST OF COLORS: *A Coach's Story*

on Kaepernick, who, by the way, didn't even vote that November.[18]

But other familiar faces in football were ready to comment about protesting during the national anthem.

Former congressman and NFL Hall of Famer Steve Largent said, "That's a moment as a player to stop, reflect, and acknowledge that there's been a lot of sacrifices made to get us to a point in this country, even to have the opportunity we have as players to play this game, be paid as much as we do, and everything else. Taking a pot shot at some cause, whatever it is, during the national anthem is inappropriate."[19]

Coach Mike Ditka, one of only two people in NFL history to win a league title as a player, an assistant coach, and a head coach, told a Dallas radio station, "If they don't like the country, if they don't like our flag, get the hell out. I have no respect for Colin Kaepernick. He probably has no respect for me; that's his choice. My choice is that I like this country, I respect our flag, and I don't see all the atrocities going on in this country that people say are going on."[20]

Unfortunately, the media wasn't giving much print or airtime to guys like Largent and Ditka. They were more interested in covering the kneelers and building a national narrative against law enforcement. Police were to blame, the protesters said, and they wanted cops to stop killing black men and boys.

By February 2017, tensions were high around Super Bowl LI, where the New England Patriots and the Atlanta Falcons would face off at NRG stadium in Houston, Texas—just thirty miles from where I coached the V&P Sharks.

The Guardian predicted that Houston would see pregame protests by members of Black Lives Matter, religious leaders, and the local Democratic Party against President Trump's suspended travel ban and "a range of racial and religious issues."[21]

On game day, demonstrators from Black Lives Matter and the ACLU did show up to march against social and political injustice, and Al Green, a Democrat representing the 9th Congressional District of Houston, was among them. (He was reportedly the first member of Congress to call for the impeachment of President Trump.)

"The protest is happening today because there's injustice today," Green said. "The protest is happening here because there's injustice here. Dr. King reminded us that injustice anywhere is a threat to justice everywhere." He added, "Dr. King said, 'The right time to do right is always right now,' and I'm paraphrasing."[22]

Green was paraphrasing. Dr. King's actual quote was used in his sermon titled, "Remaining Awake Through a Great Revolution," which I've read in its entirety. The section with the line that Green attempted to quote talks about how the progression of humanity requires hard work and working together to help time rather than wait on it, and understanding that time is always "ripe" in relation to doing what's right.[23]

On February 5, 2017, I refused to watch Super Bowl LI on television, but more than 111 million people did.[24] Thousands more attended the game, paying an average of $5,000 per ticket.[25] All said and done, this single NFL event dropped

$347 million into Houston coffers.[26] Interestingly enough, no players knelt during the anthem on that high-dollar day.

As disgusted as I was with the NFL for allowing its players to kneel and disrespect the national anthem and the flag, I was far more concerned with how the media's glorification of it was affecting young athletes. On high school fields around the country, teen athletes were imitating the pros by taking a knee during the anthem at their local games, and several received media attention.[27]

It's funny how much can change in a school year. In 2016, it was perfectly fine for football players and coaches to kneel in protest *before* a high school game, but in 2015, kneeling in prayer *after* a high school game could cost a coach his job. Just ask Coach Joe Kennedy.[28]

In the six months since Kaepernick first sat down, none of the boys on our team had ever once said anything to me about him or his protest. I hadn't heard one word from any of our players or their parents about the kneeling or the reasons behind it. But I talked to them about it. I wanted the young men I coached to know how I felt about this country, about the American flag, and what it stood for. They knew that I had served in the Marine Corps, and that I had friends who had seen combat in the fight for freedom. Yes, I told them, part of American freedom is the freedom to protest, but not during the national anthem.

Not when veterans are at the game — some standing, best they can, at attention, with old hands over big hearts. Not when families, who know what it is to be handed a folded flag on behalf of a grateful nation, are considering the only colors that carry the memory of their loved ones. And not when, for just one uninterrupted stanza of national pride and patriotism, we stand together as Americans.

Several times during those kneeling months I made it clear to our boys: "Every player on this team will stand during the national anthem. There will be no kneeling. Any player who does will no longer be a Shark."

I also made it clear how proud I was of them for playing with heart, class, and respect—that's the vision I had for my football program when I started the team five years earlier. I loved coaching these boys, and I always considered it an honor to watch them improve as football players and as young men.

"All of your hard work is paying off," I told them. "Next season, the state title is well within our reach, and every team in this division knows it."

As for the national kneeling issue, I prayed that it would end with the current football season. Unfortunately for me, it was just getting started.

CHAPTER 4

THE PROTEST

⟿

I n the fall of 2017, the NFL was still taking a knee. Players continued using their nationally publicized and highly paid platform to protest during the national anthem, and fans reached a new level of frustration. Viewership of NFL games suffered, along with ticket sales, especially after President Donald Trump chimed in on the issue.

At a September rally in Huntsville, Alabama, the president said, "Wouldn't you love to see one of these NFL owners, when somebody disrespects our flag, to say, 'Get that son of a b— — off the field right now. Out. He's fired. He's fired!' You know, some owner is going to do that. He's going to say, 'That guy that disrespects our flag, he's fired.' And that owner, they don't know it. They don't know it. They'll be the most popular person, for a week. They'll be the most popular person in this country."[1]

The president went on to say, "But you know what's hurting the game more than that? When people like yourselves turn on television and you see those people taking the knee when they are playing our great national anthem.

The only thing you could do better is if you see it, even if it's one player, leave the stadium, I guarantee things will stop. Things will stop. Just pick up and leave. Pick up and leave. Not the same game anymore, anyway."[2]

The liberal media, still shocked and bruised by Donald Trump's victory in the 2016 election, used his words, in my opinion, to pit professional players against him and everything that he stood for — making America great again. He stood for the flag, so they knelt. He backed law enforcement, so they blamed police. Clearly, this was about more than football.

With the president's comments still churning the news cycle, and the comments Rhonda had made at the THESA game still fresh in mind, I felt the need to address the kneeling issue again with our boys. On Thursday, the night before our game against Providence Classical, I told the team, "Listen, I want to make it clear, we do not do any protesting during the national anthem, and anybody who does will be off the team. That's the end of your days as a Shark."

After my talk, the players went to warm up — all except for CJ and Larry. They just stood there for a moment. Then Larry looked at his cousin and said, "Let's go, CJ," and they joined the other players.

I woke up Friday morning and saw a text from Cedric, CJ's dad.

When I called him back, he said, "Coach, you know, Larry and CJ, they heard what you said last night at practice, but they feel real strong about this social injustice thing, and I think they might want to show their support by protesting at the game tonight."

"Well, Cedric, you know I'm not gonna back down on this. There's no sense in them blowing their whole season and a chance for a state title, for them and all the rest of the boys, over this. Let me give them another opportunity."

I supported the boys' right to protest, but not this way — not any way that hurt people. And I felt this degree of shameful disrespect was just as hurtful to people as protests that result in the burning, looting, and destruction of property. I was not about to support this kind of anti-American protest on my team, but I did suggest some alternatives.

"How about they kneel in the end zone after every touchdown?" I said. "I'll even put an ad in our home football program that explains why they are kneeling during touchdowns."

I'd also heard that CJ had written a term paper for school about social injustice, so I offered to print copies of it, at my own expense, and hand them out to people at our football games.

"Yeah, I don't know, Coach. They seem set on doing this, but I'm not gonna waste the gas to come out there if they get kicked off the team right after."

"Well, it will be a waste of gas if they kneel. But they don't have to do that. We can work something else out. You know me, man, we've always gotten along. You know I love these boys, and we can work something out. Have the boys call me. Better yet, have them come by my office."

Cedric agreed that the boys would come see me, so I waited for them at the church for more than two hours. But the boys never showed. Finally, I got CJ on the phone.

"Do you understand what will happen if you do this, son? You want to blow everything over this? The only thing that's going to change is that you won't be playing football after tonight."

CJ was quiet, but I knew he was listening.

"So are we good, CJ?"

There was a long pause on the phone before CJ mumbled, "Yeah, okay."

I spent the rest of the afternoon going over plays for the game. Had I checked my social media, I would have seen some of the posts that CJ and Larry put up, announcing their intent to kneel that night.

Later on, we all met at the church like we normally do before traveling to away games. CJ and Larry showed up in their own car, which was unusual for them, and despite the September heat, they stayed in the car instead of getting out and talking with the rest of the team.

Coach Wilson went over and talked to them, and he helped CJ fix his shoulder pads—an indication that he intended to play in the game.

"They were both cordial," Brad told me, "but definitely not acting themselves. They wouldn't look me in the eye, but when I asked them if they were good to go, they said yes."

I pulled both of my assistant coaches to the side and told them what was stirring in my gut. "I have a feeling that CJ and Larry are going to kneel tonight during the anthem. If they do, make sure they don't leave with our equipment."

On the field, we started the boys on warm-ups, throwing passes and blocking drills. As I always do, I walked up to each of the players and talked to them—my way of seeing how the boys feel and whether they might start the game sluggish or fired up.

I came up to Larry, who was throwing the ball to CJ, and said, "We got a deal, right? We're good tonight?"

Larry shrugged—his usual response to questions.

I asked CJ the same question and got a similar reaction.

Then I took a few minutes, as I always did, and headed to the end zone. Like my hero coach, Paul "Bear" Bryant always did at the University of Alabama, I leaned against the goal post. I'm not sure what Coach Bryant thought about as he watched his team, but I used that time to pray.

After removing my hat, I said, "Thank you, Father, for the privilege to coach these fine young men and to be here, on this field, coaching. Please protect all the players on both teams, and let us play to the best of our ability. Let all of us represent You well tonight, Lord." And while I never prayed to win a game, I would ask for the other team to lose. That night, with my heart heavy with concern, I added, "Lord, please move on the hearts of CJ and Larry to keep our agreement and not kneel."

Before the national anthem started, the announcer for the home team asked everyone to stand for prayer. I stood in front of my team; they were lined up on the sideline behind me. As I removed my hat to pray, I saw Larry take a knee, and my heart sank. All I could think was, *Dear Lord, no.*

I held a false hope that maybe he was kneeling for the prayer and just trying to give me a good scare as a joke. Surely he would stand up before the anthem started. In my heart, I prayed, "Please let him stand up." To myself I mumbled, "Please don't do this, Larry. Please don't do this."

The prayer ended, and Larry was still on one knee. From that point on, it seemed like everything moved in slow motion as the national anthem started to play.

O say can you see, by the dawn's early light,

What so proudly we hailed at the twilight's last gleaming,

I stood there, shaking my head as if we had just suffered our biggest loss. What the NFL had allowed to start — these demonstrations of disrespect — was now playing against my team, and I was seeing with my own eyes that not all boys can stand under such pressure. On one knee, a player of mine had brought down his team, his coach, and an entire football program built on the back of honor and respect.

My heart was broken. Larry was the one kneeling, but I felt like I was the one who had let America's colors fall — on this field, on my watch, on my team. I was ashamed and embarrassed for every veteran who had ever served, fought, and died for our great nation. I wanted to crawl under something and hide in shame as I thought of the families who were in the stands — the moms, dads, and children — some of whom I knew had seen our glorious flag draped over the coffin of a loved one.

Whose broad stripes and bright stars through the perilous fight

O'er the ramparts we watched, were so gallantly streaming?

Every boy on my team had heard me say, many times, why I stood for the flag, but Larry had never shared with me his desire or need to kneel. So I didn't know what he felt in his heart when his knee touched the ground. Earlier that morning I'd waited two hours for him to come and tell me, and discuss some alternative ways to protest that I had suggested. I was ready to listen. I wanted to understand. But this, how he was doing this, I couldn't understand or accept.

And the rocket's red glare, the bombs bursting in air,

Gave proof through the night that our flag was still there,

I turned my head just enough to see CJ, who was standing a little further down the line, raise his fist high in the air to form the black power sign.

My heart broke again. CJ, one of my son's best friends — or so I thought — who had spent the night at my own home with my family. The young man whom I had taken to football camps over the summer. The kid who had texted me like I was one of his friends. CJ, the one, I said privately to my wife, was one of my favorite players.

When he had confided in me that playing college football was his dream, I worked behind the scenes toward getting him a scholarship because I loved him, and I wanted to see him succeed. CJ, the one who tweeted on my birthday, "To the best coach you could ever ask for."

O say does that star-spangled banner yet wave

O'er the land of the free and the home of the brave?

I took a deep breath and then did what I had said I would do.

I walked straight over to Larry, looked him square in the eye, and shook his hand. "Larry, thank you for your time as a Shark, but your days as a Shark are done."

I tried to reach out to him, for his arm, but he pulled away from me.

I saw CJ and said, "What, are you done, too?"

CJ nodded and mumbled something.

I pointed across my chest to the field house and told both of them, "I need you to change out of your uniforms." In my mind, it was clear that my intent was for them to change in the field house restroom where I pointed. "And I need you to leave my equipment here," and pointed to the ground next to the benches. My concern was that they would leave the field with my equipment—the uniforms, helmet, shoulder pads, and jerseys cost roughly $600 per player.

Since the referees were ready to start the game, I walked back over to the sideline where the rest of players were standing. I could tell that the boys were shocked by the protest, and the fact that we were suddenly down by two players. I clapped my hands together and said, "Let's shake off what just happened, boys, and focus on the job at hand." I was saying that to myself just as much as I was telling them.

The Sharks were distracted that night, but they somehow managed to play past it. They hit hard, ran fast, caught balls, made plays, and ended up winning against Providence Classical. I was extremely proud of them, but our victory was overshadowed by the earlier protest. On the drive back to Crosby, all I could think about was Larry and CJ.

I got home close to midnight, and as soon as I got settled, my cell phone rang.

"Is this Coach Mitchem from Victory & Praise Sharks?"

"Yes, sir."

"This is Adam Coleman from the *Houston Chronicle*, and I want to ask you a few questions if that's okay. Did you remove two players from your team tonight?"

I know it sounds naive, but I thought he was just asking me questions. I didn't realize I was already being quoted for a news story.

At one point, Mr. Coleman asked me why I thought it was necessary to cut the boys from the team.

"I'm a former Marine," I said. "That just doesn't fly, and they knew that. I don't have any problem with those young men. We've had a good relationship. They chose to do that, and they had to pay for the consequences."

"Did you make them take off their uniforms?"

"Yes, sir," I answered, thinking of how I had told the boys to change out of their uniforms and leave them and their equipment by the rest of the gear near the benches.

In the coming days, I would see Larry on more than one newscast saying that I had him and CJ "script [sic] down in our uniform — pads, the pants, and all in front of everyone."[3]

Had the *Houston Chronicle* bothered to interview any of our team parents who had witnessed that particular piece of the story, they would have heard another point of view.

Alex Richmond, who saw the whole thing from his seat on the bleachers five feet away said, "Those boys decided on their own to remove their uniforms on the sideline. Their families were standing behind all of us cheering and high-fiving one another."

The publication also failed to get reaction from any of the other players. Several of them were angered by the protest, not only because it was unpatriotic, but also because it meant the automatic dismissal of two players which jeopardized the team's chances to win the state title.

Instead, the *Houston Chronicle* interviewed Rhonda, who said, "I'm definitely going to have a conversation because I don't like the way that that was handled. But I don't want them back on the team. A man with integrity and morals and ethics and who truly lives by that wouldn't have done anything like that."[4]

Coleman paraphrased the better part of "my side" of the story, but he gave his readers—and the world—one more quote from Rhonda. She said, "Actions speak louder than words. So, for him to do what he did, that really spoke volumes, and I don't want my kids or my nephew to be around a man with no integrity."[5]

I found it interesting that the *Houston Chronicle* was able to interview, write, and post this story online within a few hours. It's almost as if they had some sort of heads up.

By Saturday morning, multiple media outlets had picked up Coleman's story, reprinting their own interpretations of his third paragraph that said that I "instructed them to take off their uniforms"[6] and Rhonda's disgust of the whole thing.

From that point on, my cell phone was ringing with requests for media interviews. After reading the initial stories and knowing how the liberal media would treat me, I was careful about which interviews I agreed to do. One reporter I did speak with was Todd Starnes, and I'm glad I did because he got it right.

He opened his story with, "Ronnie Mitchem follows the teachings of Jesus Christ" and included a quote from my Facebook page[7] that I wrote defending myself against what the media was misreporting.

The quote Starnes used from my Facebook post read, "As Americans we have one common thread and that is that men and women of all color have fought and died to give us the right to live free and get to play football on a Friday night and all the other liberties we have. To disrespect that is not right."

I also appreciated the way that Mr. Starnes ended his article. In response to Rhonda's statement about not wanting CJ around "a man with no integrity," Starnes wrote, "That's too bad — because Ronnie Mitchem is the kind of football coach — the kind of preacher — who can turn undisciplined young boys into fine, upstanding young men."[8]

Unfortunately, the article by Mr. Starnes would be the only fair report to surface all weekend.

Just as my story was reaching the desks of national conservative voices like Sean Hannity, the country's interest turned, and rightly so, to Las Vegas, where a gunman opened fire on a crowd attending a music festival. Fifty-eight people were killed and hundreds more were injured.[9]

Locally, the *Houston Chronicle* continued taking jabs at me. In an article titled, "King Solomon's Mind: Coach Oversteps His Bounds with Protest Banishment," staff writer Jerome Solomon wrote: "Cedric Ingram-Lewis raised his fist; Larry McCullough knelt. Oh my God, what egregious transgressions those are. Good Lord, something must be done to these heathens. Give me a break. I know high school football coaches are gods in this state—I've written some near-worshiping odes to a few myself—but Mitchem, who is a combination head football coach and pastor, did not make the best use of his power in this case. He should be ashamed for not setting a better example for the young men on his football team."[10]

Solomon went on to thank me for my military service and closed with, "but a fist that wasn't pressed against someone's face should hardly be so offensive, even to a former Marine, that it required the kids be removed from the team. And a knee taken at any time should hardly be deemed offensive at a Christian school. I repeat, a Christian school. Hey, Victory and Praise Christian Academy . . . what would Jesus do?"[11]

CHAPTER 5

DanDee's

~

I n my lifetime, America has changed drastically in some ways, and in others, its attitudes are still the same.

I was born in Fort Walton Beach, a small city in the Florida panhandle, in late spring of 1966—a year, interestingly enough, of protest.

It was a turbulent time for America. Protesters were still marching in large numbers against the Vietnam War. Of course, a lot of those marches happened in places like New York, San Francisco, Denver, and Atlanta, but our small community kept a careful eye on the headlines printed in the local paper, *The Playground Daily News*, and we were all ears when Walter Cronkite spoke to us every night on TV. Funny, I can still hear his famous line, "And that's the way it is."[1]

Along with protests of the war, the Civil Rights movement was shaking the nation, and the result was new legislation. Just two years before, when President Johnson signed the Civil Rights Act of 1964, he said:

The purpose of the law is simple. It does not restrict the freedom of any American, so long as he respects the rights of others. It does not give special treatment to any citizen. It does say the only limit to a man's hope for happiness, and for the future of his children, shall be his own ability. It does say that there are those who are equal before God shall now also be equal in the polling booths, in the classrooms, in the factories, and in hotels, restaurants, movie theaters, and other places that provide service to the public.[2]

Two weeks after the president signed this act into law, the Harlem riot broke out after a white New York police officer shot and killed a black teenager.[3] Likewise, just days after the Voting Rights Act of 1965 became law, the Watts riot broke out in Los Angeles, triggered by the drunk driving arrest of a black man by a white California Highway Patrol officer.[4]

Also around this time, in the world of sports, fans took sides over Muhammad Ali, who used his platform as a professional athlete to protest the war. The famed boxer refused to be inducted into the armed forces. Ali's quote, printed on the 1967 spring cover of *Freedomways: A Quarterly Review of the Negro Freedom Movement* says, "No, I am not going 10,000 miles to help murder and kill and burn other people simply to help continue the domination of white slave masters over the dark people the world over. This is the day and age when such evil injustice must come to an end."[5]

So a lot was happening in America when my parents started raising their family in Florida. To be honest, they were fighting a war of their own, one that ended their marriage not long after my sister, Rhonda, and I were born. Whenever I asked questions about why they split up, Momma, in her protective way, would wrap up all of their problems in the words, "Your Daddy was a hard man." She didn't want to tell me, at least then, that my father was abusive.

Through the years, I learned from other relatives as much as I could about my father. One story seemed to set the stage for his drinking and mean ways.

As a small boy, he and his sister, Charlene, were playing in the house, chasing each other around, as kids do. Charlene had some money, and my dad was teasing her saying, "Gimme that money!" Earlier that day, a neighbor had returned a borrowed shotgun belonging to my grand-father, and somehow the loaded gun was left on the bed in my grandparents' bedroom. While playing their game of chase, my dad and Charlene ran into that bedroom. Dad saw the shotgun and grabbed it, in play, telling Charlene, "I said, gimme that money!" She laughed and said, "Never!" Dad didn't know the gun was loaded and pulled the trigger. My dad shot and killed his sister that day. Afterward, he was never the same.

In those days, families didn't get any kind of counseling or help for such things. They held the hurt in. I don't think my grandmother, Granny Mitchem, ever really forgave my dad for what he did. She always treated him differently from her other sons.

Since I never really got to know my dad, I counted on Momma. She eventually remarried, and my stepdad, Danny, was good to her and to my sister and me. His family roots were in Montgomery, Alabama, and when he got the opportunity to buy a small grocery store with his dad, Danny and Momma moved us to Montgomery.

That was 1976 — America's Bicentennial. As a ten-year-old boy, I was interested in the Freedom Train, a red, (silver) white, and blue locomotive that traveled across the country. Its twenty-six display cars were filled with more than five hundred American artifacts including Joe Frazier's boxing trunks, Judy Garland's dress from *The Wizard of Oz,* the original Louisiana Purchase, Martin Luther King's pulpit and robes, a moon rock, and George Washington's copy of the Constitution.[6]

It came closest to us on Memorial Day weekend when it stopped in Birmingham, about ninety miles away. But we didn't get to see it. My folks were focused on getting their grocery store up and running. The economy was still recovering from recession, something voters would think hard on that November.

They named the store DanDee's — a blend of my stepdad's first name, Danny, and his daddy's first name, Deeward. Momma said when they first got it, the store was in pretty rough shape, and it took them about two years to really get it going. They stocked fresh meat, dairy, canned goods, and, of some interest to me at that time, Pop Rocks candy.

Keeping prices low and quality up was the goal at our small store. It was located in a neighborhood that was about 90 percent black, maybe more, just a few blocks down from where Rosa Parks refused to give up her seat to a white man on a crowded bus.

But the color of our customers made no difference to my family. I was raised to treat everybody with respect—and I mean *everybody*. I was taught to say, "Yes, sir," and "No, ma'am," and if I didn't, there were consequences. I started working in the store when I was ten, and if my stepdad even thought I was rude to a customer, he would take me in the back room and give me a whipping. My parents weren't abusive, but they were disciplinarians; that's just the way I was raised.

That's why, even today when I look at people of color—especially as a Christian—I look at them as souls, as individuals. I grew up watching my mom treat our friends, neighbors, and customers with nothing but respect and love.

At night, things could get a little rough in that neighborhood. I remember when the owner of the store next to ours was shot, but that man did have a reputation for being ugly to people. We never got robbed at gunpoint, I believe, because we always treated everybody with respect. Still, the people we served didn't have much, and at times, they were desperate.

I remember when some of our customers told Momma that they had seen a boy, about fourteen years old, digging for food out of our store's garbage cans at night. She told those neighbors, "Tell him to come by the store, around the back (she didn't want to embarrass him), and I'll give him something to eat." Several times, Momma made him up a sandwich and a glass of milk.

The kids in our neighborhood had little or no money to spend, and there were times when the temptation to take from our store was too great. I remember some little boys who were partial to cold Grapeade. They would come into the store and slowly make their way to the coolers, open a carton of Grapeade and take turns drinking from it.

Momma, who missed nothing that went on in that store, saw them and said, "Now boys, you can't be doing that; it's stealing." They immediately started begging her not to tell their mommas, aunties, or grannies what they had done. She said, "I won't tell on you, but I want you boys to do something for me to make up for the Grapeade you drank. After school tomorrow, you come by and pick up the papers and bits of trash in front of the store." Relieved that no one else would ever find out, the boys were happy to pick up the few bits of paper that blew in from the street.

Afterward, Momma told them, "You boys are all paid up now, but if you will promise to go to church, I will give you some Grapeade and a cookie every day after school."

They agreed and went to church. But a few weeks later, one of the boys told Momma, "Ms. DanDee (that's what they called her) I ain't going back to that church no more. It takes tooooo loooong, and I'm so tired of praying to that white God."

Momma asked, "Why do you think God is white?"

"Because all you white folks—y'all have everything, and we have nothing."

Momma smiled. I think she could relate to what he was saying. She, too, had once been young and poor, although she didn't realize the poor part.

When she was a small girl, her family worked on a dairy farm, so she learned about hard work at an early age. She told me how one of her jobs on the farm was to open and close the big metal gate each time the owner drove in or out—a man, by the way, who was large and well-fed.

One day, as the owner pulled up to the gate, Momma and her sister opened it for him and as he rolled his truck through, he flipped a dime out to her, like it was nothing. The silver coin landed in the dirt by her feet. In a sharp tone that would have gotten her in big trouble with her momma, she said, "You flipped this coin out to me, but one day I'll have coins to flip back at you." This man's casual and silent gesture, in her mind, reduced my mother's worth to ten cents, and it hurt her pride. She decided, then and there, that she would work her way up in life, and that's exactly what she did.

Working hard changed her circumstances, and that work ethic is something she modeled for me, my sister, and for the few employees at the store. If my stepdad paid somebody to mop the floor, Momma would tell that worker, "You run the register." Then she would go and mop the floor instead. In fact, Momma would do jobs that other people wouldn't do— anything to keep DanDee's clean and efficient.

She did so well that a city official took notice of our store.

One day, a nice-looking and well-dressed black man came in and "informed" Momma that she was going to donate a case of whole chickens.

"Is this for a church event?" Momma had no problems helping out the local churches with raffles and such.

The suited man, who never did identify himself, shook his head no.

"Well then, I'm sorry, sir, but we're not in a position to give out free groceries, not without receiving a receipt to show what organization or charity requested the donation."

The man left the store, and my parents threw each other a puzzled look.

The next day, picketers — all young people — were outside our store, holding signs that read, "Don't Shop at DanDee's."

Momma knew most of the young people carrying these signs and asked, "Why are you picketing our store?"

They looked at her, puzzled.

One teenage boy stopped and said, "Ms. DanDee, we wouldn't do that to you. We're trying to help you."

Shortly after that, the local radio station got wind of the picketing and requested that someone from the store call in to the program to find out what the protest was about.

Momma called in and said, "I have no idea why they're picketing."

As the incident picked up more public interest, Momma and Danny went downtown to city hall. When they found the right office, they also found the same well-dressed man who had demanded the case of free chickens from their store.

He could easily get the picketers to stop, he said. "But from now on," he pressed, "when we come in and ask you for something, you're going to give it to us."

Momma, in her respectful and Christian way, said, "No, sir. Not without a receipt. I'll close the store before I give you free food."

That city official stared eyeball to eyeball with my momma, and he must have seen that she meant what she said. Closing the store would hurt the community, and he knew it, so he backed off.

At some point during that meeting, Momma learned how that official had convinced those young picketers — many of whom did not know how to read — that they were advertising for DanDee's and not protesting against it.

When Momma got back to the store, the picketers were still out there, hot from the sun. She brought them out sandwiches and cold drinks. "Y'all must be hungry," she said.

More than forty years later, when I was threatened by those who supported kneeling during the national anthem, I asked Momma what she thought about my decision to stand.

She said, "Son, it breaks my heart to see you go through this. But to me, what's happening now is the same as what happened all those years back with those picketers in front of the store. The two boys on your team who protested during the national anthem — they didn't even know what they were protesting about. Someone is telling them it's for one thing, when it's really for another."

CHAPTER 6

ACCEPTANCE

W hen you're a preacher, it's not unusual for people to ask, "When did you get *the call?*" I don't know how it is for other ministers of the gospel, but for me, God's call to preach was something I just always felt my whole life.

In the Bible, we see God calling men of all ages and circumstances. He told Jeremiah, *"Before I formed thee in the belly I knew thee; and before thou camest forth out of the womb I sanctified thee, and I ordained thee a prophet unto the nations."* After forty years in the desert, from the midst of a burning bush, God called Moses to deliver the children of Israel. And Jesus, walking by the Sea of Galilee called out to Peter, *"Follow me, and I will make you a fisher of men."*

My heart, for whatever reason, has always been turned toward God. For as long as I can remember, I've always been interested in Him, always took Him at His Word, and always loved God.

Momma tells of an Easter Sunday, when I was just a year and a half old, and she wanted her baby boy dedicated to the Lord. Ashamed of our family circumstances at the time,

Momma didn't want to explain to a pastor why her husband wouldn't be there as the head of their house to stand beside her and watch the pastor lift up their son to the Lord while they made a parental promise, in front of God and the church, to raise up their boy in the fear and admonition of the Lord.

Alone or not, Momma wanted it done. So that Easter Sunday, she found the right time and place and, with her own arms, she lifted me up and dedicated me to the Lord. Among her promises to Him concerning me, she added, "Lord, leave him on this earth a long time, and let him be my sunshine."

But as all mommas know, the weather in children changes quickly, and not every day is sunny.

Like most little kids, part of my daily routine was watching cartoons. Rhonda would usually watch with me, but I remember one morning when I couldn't rouse her in time for *Bugs Bunny*; she wanted to sleep.

"Sissy, come watch with me!" I insisted, rocking her shoulder from side to side. But all I got was a muffled "Nooooo!"

Switching tactics, I tugged on one of her long ponytails but still no response.

That was it. I was mad.

"Sissy, you come watch, or I'll get Momma's scissors and cut off your hair!" (An idea innately planted into the psyche of every young child.)

Rhonda, used to my threats to get my way, ignored me, which suddenly infuriated my four-year-old self.

So, I went and found Momma's sewing scissors, held up my sister's ponytail by the tip, and carefully laid the thick end between the blades. With one loud snip, I cut the whole thing off.

The sound of the scissors made both of us jump.

Rhonda sat up quick and grabbed the side of her head to feel the prickly sprout of cut hair. Then she started screaming and crying.

Momma rushed in to find me standing next to Rhonda's bed with the scissors in one hand and ten inches of my sister's hair in the other. For a minute, Momma just stood there, wearing a face that looked, to me, like it could break out into laughter at any second. I thought I'd help her along and threw her one of my irresistible Ronnie smiles. Boy, did I misread that one.

"You think this is funny, young man?" This was the kind of Momma question you dared not answer. In what seemed like one fluid motion, she grabbed the scissors and hair from my hands and pulled me to the other side of the room where she sat down on my bed. This is when I realized the seriousness of my crime. For most infractions, Momma spanked me standing up. But if she took the time to sit down and put me across her lap, I knew I was going to be there a while.

Rhonda, who usually took some satisfaction in seeing justice served on me, was still crying about her hair, even later that morning when Momma tried to fix it, best she could. In Rhonda's kindergarten class picture, taken shortly after "the incident," she was the only girl with a Pixie cut.

Orneriness and all, between God pulling on my heart and Momma's prayers, I was bound to be a preacher. Even as a young boy, I felt the Lord drawing me to His Word.

I remember going to the five-and-dime store, and while other kids were eyeing toys and candy, I zeroed in on a small Bible that you had to unzip to open. To this day, I don't know why a seven-year-old kid who didn't even go to church would want such a thing, but I wanted that Bible bad. Momma bought it for me, and it was my first real introduction to God's Word.

I started reading it and was happy to find it full of adventure, war, loyalty, and God's love—all the things that appealed to my little-boy heart. Soon, all those Scriptures and verses became too much to hold inside, and I felt the need to preach.

Oftentimes, after school, with Momma and Danny still at work, I would mentally convert the living room into a sanctuary. Our two dogs, Laddie and Bambi, were my faithful, if not uninterested, followers. They'd watch me set my Bible down on a TV tray pulpit and adjust the handle on our upright vacuum cleaner handle—my mic—which I grabbed and dragged, dramatically, around the room as I preached on the need for sinners to be saved. From time to time, my sister Rhonda would pass by my "church," and I'd let her know just how hot hell really was.

Again, I'm not sure where this came from because at that time, we were what you called CEOs (those who attend church on Christmas and Easter Only).

But even though we only went to church once in a blue moon, I always had a love for the Lord. I read my Bible a lot and "preached" behind my pulpit with great enthusiasm.

At the dinner table, Danny, who was not a church guy, always asked me to bless the meal. Since my oratory skills were still being honed, I'd mumble out something short and quick as in, "Lord, bless this food. Amen."

But one day, in the back of my Bible, I found some fancy prayers printed. They sounded much better than mine, so I decided to memorize one. A few nights later, when Danny asked me to pray, I recited: "Dear heavenly Father, we thank Thee for the nourishment that You have provided to sustain us in our daily commitment and devotions to following Thee. Amen."

I opened my eyes and looked around. Everybody was quiet. Danny said, "Where in the world did you learn that?" I told him how I'd found the prayer in the back of my Bible and memorized it. My stepdad said, "God don't want to hear that. He wants to hear a prayer from *your* heart."

To this day, those words ring true. Whenever I see someone reading a printed prayer during a service, I think to myself, "God wants to hear the prayer that's in your heart."

In the middle of my seventh grade year, we moved to the other side of Montgomery, and Rhonda and I had to change schools. She's only a year older than I am, so that January, we started at Goodwin Junior High School, and we hated it.

It's never easy being the new kid in class, especially in junior high. I didn't know anybody. I had lost all of my old friends and was finding it hard to make new ones. Football was the only familiar thing I had to hold onto, so at practice I worked hard to show them what I could do. The coaches at my old school had played me as a starter—a nose guard on defense. But the coaches at Goodwin wanted me to move to the center position on offense. Now nothing was going right—not even football.

On the walk home, there were two guys that started talking to me a little—Steve McCloud and Glenn Cannon. They lived in Forest Hills, the same subdivision as mine. Little by little, on the walk to and from school, we became friends.

Turned out that Glenn's neighbor, Don McLeod, was a friend of my stepdad's. Our families ended up having dinner together, and the topic of church came up. When Mrs. McLeod (Nelta) found out that we hadn't found a church yet, she invited us to theirs: First Assembly of God, Montgomery.

Momma and I had tried a few local churches but hadn't found one that we really liked. Since she had grown up in the Assemblies, Momma was excited to visit this one. I had never been to anything but Baptist churches, so I really had no clue that there was a difference, but I was willing to give it a try.

On Sunday, we got dressed up and drove out to church. From the moment I stepped inside, I could feel the excitement. The people seemed so happy to be there; they couldn't wait for the service to start. When the musicians started playing and the choir began to sing, I saw people close their eyes and raise their hands in a holy reverence. At other times, they clapped, and a few people even danced. I had never been in a church like this before, and I enjoyed every minute of it.

By the time Pastor Coy Barker got ready to preach his sermon, everybody was fired up, and so was he. Pastor Barker was a tall man, and when he stepped behind the pulpit, I heard a few of the ladies whispering about how good-looking he was. Later I learned that he was from Oklahoma and was part Indian and part cowboy. In his younger days, he had even been a bull rider. I liked him immediately. To me, he was the John Wayne of preachers.

And he didn't stay stuck behind the pulpit either. Pastor Barker stepped out, like any cowboy would, and walked the whole platform, speaking in a way that held my attention. It was like I was listening with my heart, and, for the first time, I heard that I needed to be saved and washed in the blood of Jesus. I had seen altar calls given before, but now I understood that to restore my relationship with God, I had to ask Jesus into my heart. And by the end of that service, I wanted to ask Him.

But when the moment came, I was too scared to go up in front of everybody, so I stayed in my pew. All that next week, I thought hard about what Pastor Barker had preached, and I couldn't wait to go back to church.

Sunday finally came, and before I knew it, Pastor Barker was saying, "If you love God, then you have to accept His Son, Jesus. I'm going to ask you to bow your heads, with nobody looking around, and when I count to three, I want only those who want to make a commitment to Christ to make eye contact with me."

I wanted to accept Jesus bad, but I was shy and got uncomfortable when people looked at me. I knew if I made eye contact with the pastor, I'd have to stand and walk up to the front of the church in front of everyone. Surely the Lord knew what I was thinking because just then Pastor Barker said, "I'm not going to embarrass you by having you come down front. I just want you to make eye contact with me so that I know you're serious, and I can lead you in prayer." He said he would count to three and then begin praying.

The Lord was meeting me more than halfway, but I still sat there, looking down at my shoes. As the music played, I kept hearing his words from before, "If you love God, then receive the gift of His Son Jesus dying on the cross." Then I heard the pastor counting.

"One."

I did love God, I knew I did.

"Two."

And I love Jesus. I really do want Him in my heart.

"Three."

I jerked my head up and looked square into the pastor's eyes, just as mine began to fill with tears.

I stood up from the pew — without feeling shy or afraid — and repeated these words after Pastor Barker: "Lord, I love You, and I accept your gift of salvation. I ask You to come into my heart. Wash me with Your sinless blood. I repent of my sins. I believe in my heart that You are the Savior of all men. I confess You with my mouth — You are my Lord and my Savior. Amen."

Even though I was just twelve years old, it seemed like a heavy weight had been lifted from me. I felt a joy that I had never felt before. When the pastor said I was born again, washed in the blood of Jesus, and that my name was written down in the Lamb's book of life, I felt like I could fly.

Momma, who was beaming, asked, "Do you know what you just did?"

"Yes, ma'am. I just gave my heart to Jesus!"

When I got to school on Monday, I couldn't wait to tell Steve that I'd accepted the Lord, and how much I loved going to his church. And now it was my church, too, and I went every time the doors opened.

The weeks passed by, and even though I was excited about my new relationship with the Lord and was witnessing to the kids at school, I still found it hard to break some hard habits—mostly fighting.

At my old school, I had gotten into some fights. One was with a ninth-grader who was two years older than me. When Momma asked the principal why I was being suspended when the other boy started it, he said, "Because Ronnie wouldn't stop fighting. Even after we broke it up, he went back after the boy."

I did have a temper problem, something the kids at Goodwin were about to learn. One day in class, when the teacher had her back turned to write on the board, the boy sitting in front of me turned around and started talking trash to me. When he did it a second time, I said, "You turn around again, and I'm gonna slap the fire out of you." He turned around again, and I slapped him hard enough that it echoed through the classroom. Some of the kids looked shocked, and others laughed, but the teacher didn't know what had happened.

Later, in gym class, my new enemy wanted revenge. We squared off in the locker room and had a big fight. After it was over, one of the guys said, "I thought you were gonna be a preacher."

I wiped a little blood from my lip and said, "I am. But I ain't one yet."

My philosophy on fighting, then and now, goes something like this: I will never start a fight, but I won't run from one either. I will always stand up for myself, and I will always stand up for other people who are being treated wrong, no matter what. I'd rather lose a fight than be a coward. To me, being scared is a shameful thing for a man. I figure it's better to go down fighting than to let someone strip you of your pride and dignity. At least if you stand up, you can sleep at night knowing that fear didn't own you. I won't back down, couldn't force myself to back down, and can't remember a time when I ever did. I'm not a troublemaker; I never look for trouble and have never tried to start any problems with anyone. I've always tried to get along with people, but I do have a limit to what I will take.

To fix my temper problem, I knew I needed God to help me, so I started praying. The next Sunday, Pastor Barker talked about "going into your prayer closet," so I decided to give that a try. When I got home from church, I scooped up my shoes from the floor of my closet and threw them under my bed. Then, by carefully arranging a small stack of storage boxes, a pillow, and a blanket from my bed, I made a sort of chair and just like that, I had a prayer closet. Every morning and every night, I'd shut myself up in there and tell God, "Please help me not to get so mad sometimes. Please help me to be better."

I also spent time in that closet thinking about my dad. After he and Momma divorced, my real father wanted nothing to do with me. So from three years up, I never got a Christmas present or a birthday card from him. I figured all that disappointment had settled down deep inside and occasionally bubbled up as a burst of anger. Sometimes I was sad and mad at the same time. I wanted my dad to want me. I saw at school how other divorced dads showed up to see their kids and spend time with them. Why didn't my dad want me? What was wrong with me? Was he embarrassed of me? Was I too stupid or too ugly? These questions hung a lot heavier on me as I tried to find acceptance in a new school.

Momma was cleaning one day and asked why all my shoes were under the bed, and why half my bed was in the closet.

"That's my prayer closet," I said.

Momma couldn't help but laugh. "Ronnie, that's not quite what Pastor Barker meant." She looked around my room that I had decorated with posters of the Dallas Cowboys Cheerleaders, Loni Anderson, and Lynda Carter — all of them wearing the equivalent of swimsuits.

Momma pointed to my posters and asked, "Do you think Jesus would want to be in this room with all these girls dressed like that?"

I smiled and said, "Well, Momma, He did make them that way."

She gave me that "momma look" of hers and said, "You might should pray about that."

I knew Momma was right, and I decided that if I really wanted God to move in my life, I needed to show Him that I was serious. So I took down my posters, tore them up, and threw them in the trash. Then I knelt down beside my bed and prayed that God would help me to become the person that He wanted me to be. "Lord, help me to show Your love to others through my life."

CHAPTER 7

COACH WARD

In junior high, I didn't care much for school. Like most kids that age, I only wanted to do what I was good at, and I was good at football. I knew that because of my coaches. On the field, their praise made me push myself harder. Whenever I heard a "Way to go, son; good play," I treasured it. A boy takes to heart what his coach tells him. Players watch their coaches carefully—how they talk, how they live, and how they treat other people. A good coach, I learned, reaches his players at the heart, where love for the game lives.

I'd recently given my heart to God, and in it He found my heart's desire—to play college football. And I was on my way, too. In junior high, I was an all-city nose guard. But as a special gift, I believe, God put Coach Glen Ward in my life. In one person, the Lord showed me how I could serve God and play football at the same time.

When I met him, Coach was on staff at my church, First Assembly of God, and part of his job there was establishing a new Christian school. Since he had played football at Auburn University, Coach insisted that the new school, Bell Road

Christian, include a football program, and he would be the head coach. The school was to open in the fall of 1979, at the start of my eighth-grade year. I desperately wanted to go to Bell Road, but first I had to convince my parents that this private Christian school was better than public Goodwin School.

I asked Coach if he would talk to my folks about it. Without hesitation, Coach showed up at my house and talked up the school to Momma and Danny. They knew how much I loved football, and once Coach assured them that Bell Road would have a team, they agreed to make the switch.

I was thrilled. I would get to leave Goodwin and go to a Christian school where I could learn more about the Bible and play football. Later that night, I knelt down by my bed and told God, "Thanks, Lord, for letting me go to this school. I promise to do better in class, not fight, and work hard at football for Coach."

That summer, I grew a couple of inches taller both physically and spiritually. I was still a new Christian, but I felt the Lord working in my life. Not long after I was saved, I started learning bits and pieces about the baptism with the Holy Spirit—something I didn't know much about.

On a Thursday night, Pastor Barker preached on it from the book of Acts. He told about the day of Pentecost and how a mighty rushing wind filled the house where those who followed Jesus waited, just as He had told them to do.

When Pastor Barker read, *"And they were all filled with the Holy Ghost, and began to speak with other tongues, as the Spirit gave them utterance,"* something in my heart ached to know more. The same thing had happened when I heard others in our church speak in tongues during times of worship. The languages were so fluid and beautiful, you couldn't help but wonder at the sound. Somehow I knew it was God helping them to commune with Him in a most holy way.

At the end of his message, the pastor asked for those who would like prayer to receive the baptism to come forward. Dozens of people stood up and walked to the altar, some already weeping. By the time I got up my courage to step out, the altar area was so crowded that I wondered how Pastor Barker would be able to pray for all of us. I decided not to wait for him. I went ahead and asked the Lord on my own.

I lifted my hands and prayed, "Lord I don't know anything about this, but the preacher said it will bring an even a deeper love for You, and that You will be able to use me in a greater way than ever before. I love you, Lord, and I want more of You."

I was still praying with my eyes closed when I felt a hand on my head, and at that moment, I experienced what I can only describe as the love of the Lord Jesus Christ around me and through me. He baptized me in His precious Holy Spirit, and I wept as He impressed on my heart new words in a language I had never heard before. In faith, I uttered those first few syllables and phrases, and then it was like turning the handle on a faucet. Soon sentences were flowing, and I poured out to God things that had been locked up tight in my heart, and I knew He was hearing me. I was in direct contact with my heavenly Father, and I didn't want it to stop. As I cried out to Him in a language unknown to me, it was as if God was saying back to me, "I know, son. I know."

Years later, Phil and Becky Henderson and I were talking about that night, how so many people, including me, had responded to the altar call. I told her I was surprised that Pastor Barker had gotten around to everyone, laying his hands on people and praying for them to receive the baptism.

"He even laid his hand on me," I said, "and I was clear in the back of the pack."

Becky looked at me funny and then got a little teary-eyed.

"It was an emotional night," I said, seeing that she was obviously moved by the memory.

She shook her head slowly and smiled. "Ronnie, I followed you to the altar that night to support you in prayer. I was there the whole time, and no one laid a hand on you."

Some will disagree with such experiences, but I know this one to be true. I believe the Lord touched me in a special way that night, because I came away with a joy and a peace that I had never known before. I could not stop praising Him for what He had done in my life. On Monday at school, my face would not stop smiling — "like sunshine," Momma said.

Things were beginning to balance out for me — school, church, and football — and God used Coach Ward to show me how to be strong in all three. Coach constantly encouraged me to study with my head, worship with my heart, and use both to play football. I watched how he did it. In the classroom, behind the pulpit, or on the field, Coach was always the same.

I wanted to be like him that way, so at home I prayed and read my Bible. Over time, I noticed that some of the anger and sadness I felt about my dad began to break. God was revealing Himself to me through His Word and through others, like Coach. For the first time, I was beginning to understand the word *Father*.

At school, I wanted other kids my age to experience God the way I had, so I told friends — and a few of their friends — what God had done for me. I became heavily involved in sharing the gospel through neighborhood Bible clubs, and even did a little street preaching in some rough areas of Montgomery. I shared my testimony often and led a lot of kids to Christ.

Months earlier, when I started at First Assembly, I was the only kid sitting on the front row, alone. Now, the front rows on both side of the aisle were filled with young people.

I remember one Friday in school chapel when a boy from our football team responded to the altar call and gave his life to Christ. Afterward I told him, "I'm really glad you got saved."

He said, "Man, you're one of the reasons I got saved."

"What do you mean?"

"I saw that smile on your face *every day*. No matter what happens, you're always happy. I just wanted to be happy like you."

Our church leaders also took note of my evangelistic efforts. Years later, Coach Ward shared with me how much Christianity had changed me. "You were transformed," he said. "Your attitudes, words, and behavior changed almost immediately. In discipling you, it was evident you had a heart for God and began to follow Him hard. You grew quickly in the faith and were uncompromising in your convictions."

Others in church assumed I would become a preacher someday. Being in the Assemblies, I remember hearing more than once, "That Ronnie's going to be another Jimmy Swaggart."

Every Friday we had chapel services, and Coach would play his guitar, accompanied by Janet Alexander on the piano. Coach always took the time to minister to us kids, and he always seemed to know exactly what to say. I was hungry to learn more about the Bible, and Coach would always find time to talk to me and explain it in a way that I could understand.

It was the same way on the football field; Coach knew how to build his players up. At different times, he would use me as an example of being fearless — unafraid of contact. You can imagine how that made a thirteen-year-old boy feel. And he stood by what he said, starting me on varsity as a lineman (and linebacker).

The first game at Bell Road Christian was a beat down from Landmark Christian, who ran through us, over us, and around us. We were all beat up, but we were happy to have a bye week so we could heal and get ready for our next game. At practice, Coach had to leave the field to take a call in the school office. He came back, called us all together, and told us to take a knee.

"That was Landmark on the phone, boys, and the team they were going to play Friday night canceled. They want to know if we'll play them again." I'll never forget the look of doom on all of our faces. It was deathly quiet.

"I know what you might be thinking," he said, "but this is a chance to redeem ourselves. We could go and show those boys just like David showed Goliath. We can do this if we believe in each other and in ourselves."

By the time Coach got done with his speech, we were on our feet cheering and ready to go. We believed that we could do the impossible and embraced the challenge of giving Landmark a beat down. We practiced harder than usual to get ready, and when the buzzer sounded at the end of the fourth quarter that Friday night, we were still on the losing end of the scoreboard, but we felt like winners. Even though Landmark won the game (and it was a lot closer this time), we had won the respect of our opponent for taking on the challenge and fighting to the very end.

If Coach's philosophy could be summed up in four words, they would be: prepare, plan, execute, and believe.

I understood this better after a game against a team from Mobile. Coach put in a new play that he believed could be a game changer. On the field that Friday night, the score was close and time was running out. We needed a touchdown to win. More pressing was the fact that we were in a fourth and inches scenario, at about midfield. When the play was sent in, Coach had called it "The Middle Screen."

I was playing guard on offense, and as we were getting ready to snap the ball, the defense started to crowd the line of scrimmage, taunting us as if to say, "We're coming." They were selling out to stop the run, and I was thinking, "We've got you now."

When the ball was snapped, they sent everybody to stop the run. We held our block for a three count and then let them go as our fullback slipped behind the rushing defenders. Our quarterback baited them in and then dumped the football over their heads to a wide-open Robbie White, who took it to the end zone for a touchdown, and we won the game. Coach had called the perfect play at the perfect time, and the team had executed it perfectly.

From time to time, Coach would gather us on the field and remind us what it meant to be a good football player, win or lose:

> You should be respectful and teachable. Endure, if not enjoy, physical contact — you have to have mental toughness. Have heart and know the game. At all costs, you must be winners, but winning is defined as using your God-given talents to the fullest extent — doing your absolute best, spending yourself on the field, and walking away after the game, knowing in your heart that you have given everything. And, if you know you didn't give everything, purpose in your heart to do it next time. You can lose on the scoreboard and still be a winner. You can win on the scoreboard and still be a loser. Let me ask you, who is the true winner — a

genetically gifted athlete who never has had to really work hard to excel, or the athlete who is physically less gifted but works his tail off every day, plays with the heart of a champion, yet doesn't reach that level of performance? Life after football, boys, will soon reveal the real winners.

I remember when we played a Christian school from Mobile, Alabama. I got tired of the other team talking trash, so, during a timeout, I went to Coach and said, "That school claims to be a Christian school, but almost all of their players are cursing and taking God's name in vain every play."

Coach looked me square in the eye and said, "Well, the only thing you can do is witness to them."

"What? How am I supposed to do that?"

"You go out there and give 110 percent every play. Fire off the ball, get your block, and then help your teammates with their assignments. After knocking the opposing player on his butt and the play is over, you stretch out your hand, help him up, smile, and say, 'Praise the Lord.'"

I did exactly what Coach said to do, and when I reached my hand down to help up the guy on the other team, I saw a flash of respect in his eyes. When the game ended, both teams gathered in the middle of the field, and Coach asked me to lead them in prayer. After that night, Christianity and football were no longer separate things to me. I felt the same playing ball as I did witnessing to kids on the street. Both, I learned, could be done for the Lord.

People who have never played football might not understand God using a coach and football to teach a boy how to work hard, stay dedicated, and push himself when he feels like quitting, but He did. Even now, when life weighs me down, I can still hear Coach saying, "Remember, you're a team, and you're all counting on the man beside you to do his job. If everybody does his job, we are unbeatable. As long as you give your all, when you leave this field, you can sleep well tonight."

Years later, I learned that Coach wanted his players to accomplish five things each season:

1. To represent the Lord, their families, the school, and themselves in a Christlike way, honoring God and showing respect to God-ordained authority and their competitors.
2. To learn the fundamentals of the game, understand and play by the rules, exhibit self-control, and take out any frustrations with their opponents "within the whistles."
3. To win gracefully, lose humbly, and learn from both experiences.
4. To give their very best—lay it all down on the field—and walk off with their heads held high, knowing they did so.
5. To see the applications of the sport in their own lives.

I can still hear him saying, "You establish goals, work hard, discipline yourself, and don't cower to adversity but learn and grow from it. Persevere and never, never quit."

Coach would encourage us to do things that we thought were impossible. He never gave up on a player. I remember him trying to teach me the middle linebacker position—a position I had not played before—but Coach was convinced that I would be good at it because I was a hard hitter and had a nose for the football. I was known to deliver what we called "slobber knockers," which was when you hit players so hard that you caused them to slobber and snot on themselves. I was never afraid to hit. I loved hitting, which was why I loved football. I was not the fastest guy, but I could hit you. Like one of my Facebook friends recently posted, "I still have headaches from you, man." I always tell my players, when it comes to hitting, it's better to give than to receive. It's also the one time in life when you get to hit somebody and not get in trouble.

In learning this new position, I had the piece of stopping the inside run covered but struggled with stretching the play to the sideline and then delivering the tackle. Coach worked with me and worked with me.

"Just keep at it," he said. "One day it will click."

I'll never forget the night that it finally did click for me, and it could not have been set up any better. It was a fourth-and-short, and the other team decided to go for it. They ran to the wide side of the field, but I stretched the runner to the sideline and then delivered a perfect form tackle, putting the running back on his back just short of the first down marker.

The best part was that it all happened on our sideline right in front of Coach.

As I was getting up off the running back, somebody was hitting me in the head and shoulder pads. It was Coach, wearing as big a smile as when he beat Alabama in his freshman year at Auburn in the Punt Bama Punt game. (And, might I add, that was the *last* time Auburn beat Bama for ten years.)

But just like Coach said, it clicked. I believe God used Coach to show me, through football, that you can do anything if you work hard enough.

Coach Ward was and still is my spiritual dad. Even now, when I need to talk to someone, I call him, and he always finds time to talk with me. I find comfort in him telling me, "Brother, I'm going to storm heaven about this and agree with you in prayer."

If ever I needed someone storming heaven for me, it was in the fall of 2017. I remember what Coach told me when Colin Kaepernick started protesting. He said, "Well Ronnie, it's disrespectful and offensive for NFL players to kneel in protest during the national anthem. We live in the greatest country with the most freedom anywhere in the world today. Men and women have given up their lives throughout our history to give us this freedom. If they feel there are still injustices — and in some cases there are — there are more appropriate, honorable, and fruitful ways to bring about change."

My feelings exactly. Even so, when the national protest spread to players on my six-man team, I needed to know what Coach thought. He never told me what to do, but Coach agreed with my decision to remove the players from my team. Then, using personal points numbered one through four, he explained his reasons: "First, you personally invested in those young men's lives. Second, the rules were clearly stated, understood, and agreed upon. Third, you sat down with these young men, explaining your convictions, and told them you would support alternative ways of helping them with their cause and getting their message out. Fourth, you directly asked these two players if they were okay with that, and they told you they were, but their subsequent actions proved they were dishonest, disrespectful, and rebellious. Perhaps, they were influenced by outside forces. If so, they should be ashamed."

Then Coach said something I really needed to hear. "Sometimes, Ronnie, we have to suffer for doing what is right, and I admire you for your courageous stand."

Thanks, Coach, for everything.

CHAPTER 8

UNFAIR AND UNBALANCED

⟶

As a conservative, it's a hopeless feeling, dealing with the mainstream media. In my case, most of the media I dealt with wanted to hear and publish two things: that I went too far by kicking CJ and Larry off my team for demonstrating their right to protest racial injustice, and that I was cruel for making them "strip" out of their uniforms in public.

Both points were untrue.

Larry and CJ did get to protest when and where they wanted to; no one stopped them. And I did not make them remove their uniforms on the sidelines in public. Had I seen them doing that, I would have called time out and asked them to go and change in the nearby restroom or by our equipment trailer, although I thought I had made myself clear when I spoke with them after their protest, just as the game was starting.

But fair and balanced reporting was not on the agenda that Saturday, especially after the media came and saw how small my world was in this suburb of Houston. My church, small home, and our football field all sit on twelve acres.

Without the help of some of the men in the church, the football field would be just that — a field. They helped me make the goal posts, place the metal bleachers, and construct the press box that bears the words "Shark Tank." Our scoreboard was donated by a generous member of our church. As for the football field, I seeded it myself, and when the grass finally came in and grew a few inches, I mowed it myself.

So when reporters affiliated with ABC, CBS, and NBC saw the place, you could almost hear the wind going out of their sails. Where was my boss and the administrators of our expensive private school?

One reporter said, "But you're listed as Victory & Praise Christian *Academy* on the Internet."

"Yes," I said. "After we closed our Christian school in 2013, we tried to get MaxPreps to change that to Victory & Praise Christian Athletics, but after a few years of trying, we realized they were never going to change our name."

When I got blank stares, I went on. "We're a homeschool football program. We provide boys who are homeschooled or attend schools with no football program the opportunity to play football here. We don't get any funding from the state or government, and no kid has to play for us. It's completely their choice. But if they do play, they must abide by our rules."

I could tell they were still having a hard time understanding the fact that our six-man football team wasn't associated with the Independent School District or any other school entity. "None of the coaching staff receives any pay for our time and work in the program," I said. "We're volunteers," and I let that sink into their notebooks.

I also let the media know that to make the program possible, each player was required to pay $400 for the season. This fee covered insurance, uniforms, and equipment; the rest of the team's expenses came out of either my pocket or from fund-raisers and donations.

Clearly, the angle that I was some white racist coach who was set on pushing his right-wing beliefs while on the taxpayer's clock was no longer going to work. The media was well aware of the public backlash the NFL was experiencing from people who found the kneeling and fist raising (declaring black power) during the national anthem as offensive as I did. With at least three-quarters of the country on my side of the issue, the media decided to use high school players to tip the scales the other way.

So, the morning after our incident, when Larry went on camera with KPRC2 Houston and said, "He made me script [sic] down in my uniform—pads, pants, and all—in front of everybody,"[1] the story line split into good against evil. The boys were good for standing up for social injustice at the cost of their high school football careers, and I was the evil, intolerant coach and Christian who should have cut these boys a break instead of cutting them from the team, let alone shaming them by having them strip in public.

ABC News 13 added to Larry's quote about me forcing them to strip in public reporting that, "The teens said that they were humiliated; it's now created a firestorm. The incident received national attention today."[2]

In their 2:28-minute video story, ABC13 sandwiched short quotes from me between Larry and Rhonda who said, "He has like a slave master mentality, you know. If you were to go back to that when, you know, they wanted to tell us this is what you are going to do and this is *how* you do it. And if we didn't comply, then we were beating, whooped, or even possibly killed."[3]

Rhonda's "slave master" quote echoed throughout national media — a public accusation that I never got a chance to respond to.

I didn't make those boys strip on the sidelines, but Larry said I did, so that's what got aired on TV and printed online. I still have a hard time understanding why he would make up such a bold-faced lie.

To fight back, I went to my Facebook page and posted this:

> *Thanks to all of you for your support. I want to be clear that I don't have a problem with people protesting if it is done the right way. But to disrespect the flag that gives us the right to protest is the wrong way to do it. I gave the two players other ways to protest that I felt were fair. I served in the US Marines alongside men of different colors and backgrounds. My Marine drill instructors told us there was no black or white Marine, just Marine Corps green, and we would all fight for our country together. As Christians, we oftentimes have different opinions on Scripture, but the one common thread to all believers is the blood of Jesus and what He did at the cross for us. As Americans, we have one common thread, and that is men and*

women of all colors have fought and died to give us the right to live free and to get to play football on a Friday night and all the other liberties we have. To disrespect that is not right. I love these two young men – one of them has spent the night at my house, and I have taken him to football camps. He and my son are good friends. But I know, and most Americans know and understand, that if we lose that one common thread – love of country and respect for what we have – then it won't be long before we lose that freedom. Martin Luther King Jr. was one of the greatest men to ever live, and he always had the American flag in his marches and rallies. He did not hate America; he wanted America to be the greatest nation on earth, and I do not believe his dream included disrespecting our great nation and those who have died for it. Black, White, Asian, Hispanic – all have come to this great nation and many have died so that I could pastor, coach, and play football on Friday night. Though many may disagree with me, this is what I believe and, as an American, I have that right. I pray these young men across America can come to understand that there is a right and wrong way to do things. God bless America!

I denied the accusation of forcing Larry and CJ to strip out of their uniforms on the sidelines, but it was too late. The haters already had their story, and they enjoyed making me look like some cruel, hate-filled animal. This broke my heart and stung my spirit. All those hours of hard work to help these two young men succeed in life had been destroyed in an instant by a hateful lie that they started and helped to spread.

I had shown nothing but kindness to these two boys. Instead of just saying that they disagreed with me on this subject of kneeling during the national anthem, they made it personal, and it not only destroyed me, but it also destroyed the football program that I had worked so hard to build. As a pastor, I felt this football program was a part of my ministry that God had blessed me with, and I loved it. That's why I had spent countless hours building the program from scratch, just so I could be a part of teaching young men to put Christ first, work hard, be dedicated, never quit, and show respect.

Had more of the conservative news sources reached out to me on this, I believe I would have gotten out the whole truth of what happened. I could see Mike Huckabee or Sean Hannity pulling the positives from my story, such as my willingness to work with the boys to protest in less offensive ways, like kneeling in the end zone after every touchdown and printing the reason for it in the football programs. Again, it was never the protest I minded, just not during the national anthem.

But only conservatives with national audiences who covered my story were Todd Starnes in print and radio, and Frances Swaggart on her Christian network television program, *Frances & Friends* — an interview that came about from my ministry relationship with Jimmy and Frances Swaggart.

A pastor friend of mine in South Carolina, Scott Corbin, had me on his *Sound of Truth* radio program, and Chris McDonald of the McFiles news channel and the *Great Smoky Mountain Journal* interviewed me on his internet program.

I appeared on *Frances & Friends* via Skype on October 3, and the comment I appreciated most was when Frances said, "Tell us what happened to you." For the first time, I got to speak my piece without being cut short or edited.

Since her program is two hours, I was able to share with her and the panelists how the Sharks got started and how our football program was about more than just football. "We try to use the program as an opportunity to bring Christian things into the lives of these young men and talk about Christ. We have people from all different kinds of churches who play football for us. Some of them don't even go to church, but we emphasize Christ, and we make them play with class. They are not allowed to backtalk the referees or the coaches — none of that goes on in our program. It's all about teaching young men to be men."[4]

Since her show has a potential reach of some 280 million viewers worldwide over the SonLife Broadcasting Network, this interview got me the most response. Unfortunately, after it aired, it was only available in the ministry's archives for a few months, unlike the rest of the media coverage that will be online forever.

In all the reporting from ABC, CBS, CNN, NBC, Associated Press, BBC, Reuters, *The New York Times*, *Newsweek*, *The Sacramento Bee*, *Sports Illustrated*, and others, there were several questions that went unasked.

One was, as their coach, how could I make two young men strip in front of everyone if I couldn't even make them stand for the national anthem?

Second, had either of these boys actually been "humiliated" to the degree that it was reported, what parent or relative of these boys would have stood by, watched it happen, and not responded? Just the week before, at the game against THESA, Rhonda had confronted the other team's coach when she *thought* her son had been mistreated by his players. So making CJ and Larry strip in public, as I was accused of doing, surely would have warranted a similar, if not more dramatic, response from her or other family members who were at the game that night.

But the reporters I dealt with never challenged the false claim that I had made Larry and CJ strip out of their uniforms publicly on the sideline. To this day, not one person has been interviewed or asked if I made the boys strip. If the media thought this was such a humiliating act, why didn't anyone confirm that it had actually happened? Also hard to believe is that not one parent, relative, or bystander captured the protest or the alleged "stripping" with a cell phone camera or video.

Another unasked but obvious question: How did the other eleven players on my team feel about their coach's decision to cut Larry and CJ for protesting during the anthem? I coached a team of thirteen players — not just two — and eleven of them stood behind my rule of no protesting during the national anthem. In their own hearts and minds, those eleven boys believed that when "The Star-Spangled Banner" plays before a game, it's right and respectful to stand. Had I not taken action against a team rule that was broken in front of them and in front of their parents, I believe they would have left the team. (Afterward, I had parents tell me that they would have pulled their sons from the team had I not reacted the way I did.) As the coach, I had a duty to all of my players, their parents, and to those who looked to me as a leader to uphold our team's rules.

Another unasked question: Cutting two of my players for protesting automatically jeopardized the team's chances of winning a state title. What coach would do that? In high school–level football, a state title is what every coach dreams of achieving—the ultimate prize to enjoy for a lifetime. But had I done nothing in response to two of my players disrespecting the flag, and had we won the state title as the Sharks were on track to do, I couldn't have enjoyed it. Putting a title before my country—the very country that gave me the opportunity to coach a group of young men in the sport we love—was inconceivable to me. I would have never been able to wear that state title ring or display the trophy. And I would have never been able to look at myself in the mirror or enjoy another day of coaching.

But instead of asking questions like these to make their stories fair and balanced, the media believed what CJ, Larry, and Rhonda told them because that's the narrative that fit what they wanted to print and televise. The facts are, the mainstream media doesn't care about the truth, just the story, and whoever gets hurt along the way, so be it.

Denying these boys the right to protest against the opinion that black people are being routinely gunned down in America by likeminded white racist cops was every liberal reporter's dream story, and they were not going to waste this opportunity by finding out all of the facts. To the media, only two facts were necessary — the boys were black, and I was white — end of story.

Now all they had to do was feed their version to the hungry masses of America haters — people who hate facts and despise truth; people at the ready who want to march in the streets and burn, break, and destroy anything in sight because they are so filled with venomous hate.

If the mainstream media were to come clean and be honest, they would have said what they really thought of me in this situation:

> So what if somebody kills him or his family? And what do we care if his church is burned down, his ministry is destroyed, or his football program ends? We have a job to destroy anybody who dares to be a Christian or love America. Our goal is to destroy anybody and everybody who is unwilling to go along with annihilating America. What does the truth have to do with anything? This preacher-coach and former Marine — a white guy who loves America and believes in its outdated ways — with people like him around, how will we ever get rid of that racist American flag and

outdated Constitution? We don't need the truth; we just need the biased story to help us push the agenda of our left-wing bosses who care only about destroying Old America and bringing in a new one—a socialist or maybe even communist government. That way, boys like CJ and Larry will have more rights.

Yes, sir, that is the American media of today. Whoever fits their agenda is a victim, and anybody who does not go along with their agenda is destined for destruction at any cost. I was marked for destruction because I personify what they hate: someone who loves his country and believes in the American dream; someone who, as a young man, served his country as a US Marine; a guy who built a carpet-cleaning business out of the back of his Chevy Blazer into one of the best businesses in the city and then sold it to attend Bible college and eventually start up a church to preach the gospel of Jesus Christ.

I was every leftist's nightmare.

CHAPTER 9

Failure and Faith

W hen the reporters finally left, I locked up the church, walked across the football field, and climbed the wood stairs to our small press box. I needed some time alone to think and pray about all that had just happened.

I sat down in one of the chairs, exhausted. I felt drained, tired, and all alone. The cameras and microphones were gone, but the reality of all that had happened settled into my heart, and a new fear began to grow. I looked out over the football field. From here, I could see my house and the church. I thought about all that God had done for me, especially here in Crosby these past fourteen years, and I felt the sting of tears as I prayed: "God, You built this church. You brought miracle after miracle so that this church could even be here. I came here with a wife, three small children, and not a penny to my name, but You have blessed us beyond our wildest dreams. You have made a way for me every step of the way."

I've learned that at times like these, it's important to remind yourself of what God has done in your life. It builds the faith you need to ignore what the devil is about to tell you, and he's never short on words. His was the same voice I heard when we loaded up a U-Haul truck and left Florida for Texas to start this church. "You're going to lose your wife and your family," the devil promised. "Your ministry will fail."

We started Victory & Praise Worship Center in a hotel conference room, and I remember hearing the devil whisper to me, "Nobody is going to come to a hotel for church. Your ministry is done. You're wasting your time." I heard the same evil voice again when we moved the church from the hotel to a storefront: "No one will come. You're going to lose everything, and this time you won't recover."

When we first bought this property, it came with a garage that we converted into a one-room church. It had no bathroom, so we had a porta potty set up outside. Once again, I heard the devil's voice. "Nobody will come to this broken-down old building, and they sure won't use a portable toilet."

From the press box, I looked again at my house and thought about how far God had brought me. My mind went to my first days as a young preacher. Back then I lived in a Sunday school room and ate hot dogs almost three times a day, but I was happy because I was pastoring people. I saw them come to accept Jesus Christ into their lives and make Him their Lord and Savior. Now, all these years later, it seemed as though Satan was sitting in the chair beside me, and I could hear his evil voice saying, "You've really done it now. You've destroyed everything that your God has done for you, and you're going to lose it all. You and your hardheadedness. What were you thinking, trying to stand up for what you believe? What has it gotten you? Everything you're staring at right now — your home, your church, your football program — all of it will be gone, and no one will help you get it back."

Failure, real or imagined, is one of Satan's most lethal weapons against the believer.

I got saved at age twelve, but by sixteen, I had completely backslid. Our church had gone through an ugly split, so I stopped going. At home, I started noticing cracks in the relationship between Momma and Danny. Added to this perfect storm was my age, sixteen. In my mind, I was more man than boy, and I decided I didn't need church or home. What I needed was a beer, and my buddies, though shocked that I would drink, were happy to have one with me.

I was also struggling a bit at Bell Road. They had quit having football, so I decided to switch schools and go to Robert E. Lee High School, and then again to Landmark High, but their football program had fallen off of the competitive radar. Between that and my grades (I wasn't dumb, just a procrastinator who didn't apply himself academically), I started wondering if I still had a shot at playing college ball.

My hopes soared a couple of times when colleges showed interest in my performance on the field, but my stepfather saw things differently.

"There's no doubt you can play," he said, "but you won't ever *get* to play."

"What do you mean?"

"Because you won't have the grades."

I think he was trying to tell me that I needed to apply myself. But what I heard was that I was an idiot who would never play college football, and that was the seed that sank deep into my heart and grew. Just like my Christianity, my dream of playing college football was slipping away.

I should have gone to God then and asked for His help, but I didn't. When you grow up without your real dad, it's hard to trust a Father you can't see. There were so many times in my life that I wish I could have gone to my dad and talked to him, but he died when I was in my early twenties — another time when I felt like a complete failure.

By then I had served my country and worked a few jobs, but it still shook me when my aunt called to say, "Your dad is sick, and you need to come see him. He's in the hospital with cirrhosis of the liver." At first I thought maybe he was in another rehab place until she said, "No, he's dying. You've got to get down here." On the long drive to the hospital, I thought about all the times growing up when I'd felt so much anger toward my dad. On most days, given the chance, I would have punched him in the mouth. Now, all I could think of was leading him to the Lord.

I walked into the hospital room and saw him lying there, connected to a ventilator, and I got scared. What I was seeing didn't match the man I remembered as a boy — always tall, always tough, and mostly mean. Just the year before, he'd gotten into a fight with some deputies who had shown up to his house on a domestic dispute call.

They came in the living room and asked, "You coming with us, Mr. Mitchem?"

Dad didn't answer. He got up out of his chair and when he got to the kitchen, he started rolling up his sleeves.

"Mr. Mitchem, what are you rolling up your sleeves for?"

"I'm going," he said, "but not without a fight," and Dad wheeled around and punched one of the deputies so hard it knocked him into the next room. Then he lit into the others. When it was over, three of those deputies filed for workman's comp.

A few months after that, I had gone to see him, and our visit ended after he shoved a shotgun in my face and accused me and his wife of liking each other, which of course was a total lie.

Now my dad lay small and quiet. Hospital beds have a way of cutting a man down. Relatives from his side of the family were gathered around, including my granny, a Church of God holiness woman, and none of them thought much of me. I stood there, looking down at my father, his head cocked back on that ventilator, and I just couldn't do it. I couldn't pray for him. His eyes were open, and at one point his pupils flickered up and down.

An uncle said, "Ron, he hasn't done that with anybody. He's trying to tell you something." I stayed for a few more minutes and then left the room. As soon as I walked out, Dad died.

"How are you going to be a preacher," the devil whispered, "when you can't even lead your own dad to the Lord? You chickened out. You failed."

Now, more than twenty years later, I did the same thing I'd done every other time I'd heard that demonic voice: I rebuked the devil in the name of Jesus Christ and then pleaded His precious blood over my family and me. Afterward, I couldn't help but wonder why this was happening. I prayed again. "Lord, all I want to do is to preach Your Word and see people saved and their lives turned around. I just wanted to help these young boys. I never wanted to hurt any of them."

My eyes scanned the football field in front of me. How could a hundred yards of dry Texas grass and faded hash marks hold so much? But they did. I'd spent hundreds of hours on this field, coaching football and loving every minute of it. Over the years, I was privileged to have some great young men play for me. Each and every one of them were, to me, "my boys," whom I called at any given moment on the field names like "Hammer Head" or "Hot Rod." Then there were those who earned special titles: Benjamin Castillo was "Big Ben"; Clayton Gerlich was "Twinkle Toes"; Austin Roy was "Fumbelina"; and Jonathan Cheatham was "J-Man."

J-Man. He was 5'5" and weighed one hundred and twenty-five pounds soaking wet, but he was solid muscle. Every time we did blocking drills, he insisted on going up against Big Ben, who was 6'8" and three hundred pounds. And every time, Big Ben would knock him flat. From the ground, J-Man would look up at me and say, "Can I try that again, Coach?" He wasn't afraid to take on the biggest man on the field, and he believed that if he kept trying, one day he'd get the best of Big Ben.

That kind of faith had grown on this field.

As their coach, I wanted all of the boys to believe that they could come from behind and still win. Sometimes I could be pretty tough, I knew that, and I'd get onto them about giving more of themselves, and giving more to their teammates and to God. That young Marine inside me would sometimes push them to a point where they thought they couldn't run another sprint or do another drill, just like my coaches had pushed me until I learned that I was capable of much more than I ever thought possible. As a kid learns to give all he can give, in the process, he earns the respect of his entire team and his coach. Most of all, he begins to believe in himself.

I thought about our very first game—we'd won 31–30 on the last play of the game. I remember huddling them up and looking into their faces streaked with sweat (and some with blood) from a hard-fought battle. I remember telling them that night, "Dig down deep, men; dig down deep. You can do this, just give everything you have for one more play."

Afterward, from the sidelines, I saw our only senior, Mark Russell. Even though it had always been his dream, Mark had never before played in a football game, and this was his first season. That night, I watched him break through the line and tackle the quarterback as he spun to run a reverse. I saw the ball come out, and one of my players, Michael Cheatham, jumped on that ball. I will never forget that moment. I ran out onto the field jumping and lifting every kid I could into the air as we celebrated the biggest win in our program's history. We had done what few football programs had ever done—we'd won our first game, and it was a win against a powerhouse program! We went on that year to make the state playoffs and started to build a strong football program.

I also thought about Shawn Haller and how he had made an unbelievable catch in the end zone where he bobbled the ball four or five times before securing it for a touchdown.

And I thought about our times as a team, after the games, laughing after a win and sometimes crying after a loss—all of us, together.

I prayed again. "Lord, have I thrown away all of these great memories and the effects on the lives of these young men just because I can't give in to what I feel is wrong? Why do I have such strong views? Why can't I just do like the other coaches and surrender to this crazy world around me? Why do I have to be the coach who stands up, and how did this become so big that it's making national news? Lord, I need Your help, and I need Your strength to stand through this. God, You know my heart. You know that I love You more than anything. Please help me."

At that moment, I felt the Lord impress on my heart certain events in my life that had shaped me and made me who I am. He reminded me of times when I'd quit at something, didn't do the right thing, or made the wrong choices, like deciding not to play college football and mistakes I'd made as a young Marine. But God also reminded me of some times when I had stayed true to who I was and refused to back down. That's when something inside me broke, and I let the tears roll down my face as a new kind of loneliness and despair crept into my heart.

Then Lord brought this verse to me: *"For God hath not given us the spirit of fear; but of power, and of love, and of a sound mind"* (2 Tim. 1:7). I wiped the tears from my face. I knew that God was going to see me through this; I just had to stand strong and believe that He was bigger than those who were attacking me. God knew my heart, even if nobody else did, and He knew that I loved CJ and Larry.

God also knew the reason why I didn't allow the kneeling as protest. It wasn't because I hated these two black boys as the media had portrayed — I stand against anyone who would mistreat a person, just as I would stand up for any person who was being mistreated, regardless of their skin color. And the reason wasn't because I had an issue with a person's right to protest. If kneeling during the anthem had been in protest against abortion — and I'm as pro-life as they come — I would have reacted the same way.

My reason for not allowing this type of protesting was simple: I didn't want players on my football team kneeling because it was disrespectful. I wanted them to understand that you don't get respect by showing disrespect, especially when you disrespect the very thing that represents the freedom *to* protest.

One thing I know: I have to live with what I do, and if I stay true to who I am, then I can sleep well at night.

I got up from my chair in the press box, and as I started down those wooden steps, I felt the Lord speak to my heart. "I know who you are," He said, "and I know that you're hard-headed. But not many men could build what you have because they don't have what it takes to stand."

CHAPTER 10

US Marine

⟶

From a kid up, I always admired the Marines. *Sands of Iwo Jima* was my favorite John Wayne movie, especially those last two minutes when Sgt. John Stryker falls, and his men gather in low around him and read the unfinished letter he had started to his son back home. Stryker wrote, "Always do what your heart tells you is right." Then the actors look up to see five Marines and one sailor recreate the raising of Old Glory on Mount Suribachi—that iconic image of World War II. In the movie, when the flag is raised, Stryker's war-torn Marines stand to their feet, and, like so many real combat veterans, see the love, sacrifice, and devotion of their fallen brothers translate into America's colors: red, white, and blue.

From that point on, the flag and the Marines were inseparable to me. So, when I realized that I wouldn't be playing college football, I made my mind up to enlist and be part of the greatest fighting force in the world. Some tried to talk me out of it by saying things like, "Man, don't go into the Marine Corps. It's tough, and you're not going to like it." But I was eighteen and determined to serve.

I expected boot camp to be bad, and I would have been disappointed otherwise. Let's just say the Marine Corps never disappoints.

That first night, when the bus stopped at the base gate, some guards passed around an old cigar box to collect the last of any contraband—cigarettes, lighters, and chewing tobacco. Then we crossed the bridge, and I was eyeballing around to see as much of Parris Island as I could, which wasn't much in the dark. We all jerked forward a little as that tired bus eased to a stop, but we straightened up quick when a drill instructor stepped onboard. His shape, from shoulders to waist, was like an upside down triangle. All of him was slim, prim, and creased.

With his back to us, he spoke quietly with the bus driver over some paperwork, and, for a split second, I wondered if maybe some of those boot camp stories had been stretched a bit. That was the last full civilian thought I had. That drill instructor spun around and started screaming at us to get off of his !@#$!@$#@ bus and get our feet on his yellow footprints outside. We jumped so high and so fast that half of us banged our heads on the ceiling before crashing into each other trying to get off of his !@#$!@$#@ bus. I got my feet on a set of yellow footprints, the same set, I figured, that thousands of other young men like me had stood on, feeling the exact same way I did—a stomach churn of pride and terror— pride in this sacred ground where I, too, would take my first step toward becoming a United States Marine, mixed with a keen awareness that I was fixing to go through torment.

They kept us up all night, doing paperwork and such, and just after they shaved our heads and got us into cammies, I went outside and joined my platoon. Suddenly I realized that the man in front was not my drill instructor. He saw me and knew the same thing. He came at me screaming to get in the right "!@#$!@$#@ platoon." I finally found my guys, but I was terrified.

After about a week, they moved us to a three-story building. The top floor was for new recruits, the middle for guys halfway through boot camp, and the bottom for those close to graduation. I remember hustling up those stairs for the first time with my duffle bag and hearing screams from up above, "Get 'em up here! Bring 'em up here!" All of us were in total fear, wondering what was waiting for us at the top. Upstairs, they had us sit down in rows, crossed-legged, facing toward the Quarter Deck. A lieutenant gave us a brief talk that ended with, "and these are your drill instructors." That's when three of the most intimidating men I'd ever seen marched through the doors, their shoes hitting the floor in time with the pounding in my chest.

You think that you can mentally prepare yourself for Marine Corps boot camp, but you can't. It's a unique test of mental and physical endurance, and just when you think it can't get any worse, it can. It really can. The lieutenant saluted the DI in charge and said, "They're all yours, drill sergeant."

That's when they started screaming, and we started moving. They'd get up into your face, sometimes one on each side, their Smokey Bear brims pressed into your temples, and you'd better have the right answer, which, of course, none of us did. Under their charge, we were "worm" recruits, among other fine, choice words, because you're not a Marine until you graduate.

But after surviving the toughest boot camp in the world, I got to wear on my uniform for the very first time the coveted Eagle, Globe, and Anchor emblem. For a Marine, that's a big deal. I like the way Sgt. Maj. David Sommers (ret.) described it. He said, "The emblem of the Corps is the common thread that binds all Marines together, officer and enlisted, past and present . . . The eagle, globe and anchor tells the world who we are, what we stand for, and what we are capable of, in a single glance."[1]

Standing on the parade grounds, I flipped back to the day that I first talked to the recruiter, remembered raising my right hand and swearing to defend the Constitution of the United States, and then endured the hardest thirteen weeks of my life, which were mostly torment. But there were some everyday moments that I will always remember, like being so physically and mentally exhausted at the end of long days — days that started before sunup and ended in darkness with us lying in our bunks, still at attention. The last order of the day was for all recruits to sing, in unison, the "Marine Corps Hymn," a cappella. I can still hear the sound of it — our voices rolling through the barracks as we sang those historic lyrics:

> *From the Halls of Montezuma*
> *To the shores of Tripoli,*
> *We fight our country's battles*

In the air, on land and sea;
First to fight for right and freedom
And to keep our honor clean;
We are proud to claim the title
Of United States Marine.

Our flag's unfurled to every breeze
From dawn to setting sun;
We have fought in every clime and place
Where we could take a gun;
In the snow of far-off northern lands
And in sunny tropic scenes;
You will find us always on the job
The United States Marines.

Here's health to you and to our Corps
Which we are proud to serve;
In many a strife we've fought for life
And never lost our nerve;
If the Army and the Navy
Ever look on Heaven's scenes;
They will find the streets are guarded
By United States Marines.

That day at graduation, I realized that everything I stood for—love of country, devotion to duty, serving the greater good—is what Americans have always stood for.

My heart swelled with pride, and even though I was still running full steam away from God, I knew that He was with me. I also knew that if I stood still long enough, I'd hear

Him say, "You wanted to play football, and you played. You wanted to be a Marine, and you are one. When are you going to do that which I've called you to do?" That part of my life was miserable. I wasn't ready to listen to God or answer His question. I was eighteen years old, and all I could see in front of me were three years of military life with no coach to help me through any of it.

After boot camp, I was sent to Marine Corps Air Ground Combat Center in Twentynine Palms, California, where I would learn to be a field radio operator. I had chosen this military occupational specialty with the hope of getting assigned to an infantry unit—a secret maneuver I had kept from Momma and Danny who wanted me in and out of the Marines in the shortest time possible.

I graduated from radio school and was stationed at Camp Lejeune in North Carolina. Many of the guys in my unit there had already served in places like Lebanon and Grenada, and their stories made my teenage self ache to fight for my country. One of my new friends, Darrell "Dewey" Helsley, told how he had been on a ship off the coast of Lebanon on October 23, 1983, when a suicide bomber gunned his Mercedes-Benz truck loaded with a ton of explosives and crashed through several barriers before stopping in the atrium of the US Marine compound in Beirut and detonating the equivalent of more than ten tons of TNT. Force from the explosion in the barracks lifted the four-story building off the ground and created a smoke cloud that could be seen for miles. Two hundred forty-one American servicemen died that morning— two hundred twenty Marines, eighteen sailors, and three soldiers—making it the single deadliest day for the Marine Corps since Iwo Jima.[2]

Back then, I was just a kid listening to Darrell and others tell of what they heard and saw and felt. Now, their memories are American history.

Since I was a Marine during peacetime, the frustration of not getting the chance to actually fight for my country began to wear on me. This, added to my lost dream of ever playing college football, was enough to declare war on myself, and the first battle I faced was against alcohol.

One night two of my buddies and I were out drinking late, and we all decided that we needed some food because we had a morning run waiting for us back on base. In those days, it wasn't unusual for me to show up just in time to change into my PTs straight from an all-night drinking binge. So we went to our favorite diner, and when we finished eating, I said, "Hey, guys, like I said on the way over here, I'm broke, you got the check?" My buddies looked at each other and then back at me, shaking their heads and laughing. Then, just as calm as you please, they stood up and walked out of the restaurant. I sat there at the table for a couple more minutes, and when I thought no one was looking my way, I scooted for the door, not quite as smoothly as my buddies had done.

Somebody in the restaurant saw us leave without paying and called the police. When I got outside, there was no car and no buddies. But there was a patrol car in the area. From the streetlights, I could make out a hilly area up behind the restaurant with a row of backyard fences at the top. I made my way up there and laid low in the tall grass growing along the fence line. What I didn't know was, mixed in with that tall grass was poison ivy. The police were getting closer to me, so I crouched down as low as I could on all fours. In the dark I couldn't see the ground too well, but I sure felt the ants crawling on my hands and arms, some making it all the way to the back of my neck. By this time the police were close to me, out of their patrol car and on foot. Beams from their flashlights weren't ten feet from me when a couple of dogs on the other side of the fence closest to me saw me and started barking like crazy. The cops thought the dogs were barking at them, so they moved on down the street.

As soon as they left, I saw my buddies circling the block, looking for me. I flagged them down, and they slowed the car just enough for me to run alongside and dive into the back seat. We got about a block down the road when a cop car stopped us. I acted like I was passed out, but the cops made all of us get out of the car.

The officers were talking among themselves, discussing whether or not we were the guys they were after, and for some reason, even though I'd never smarted off to a police officer before, I told them what I thought of their "discussion" about us. Without missing a beat, they told me I had the right to remain silent. All three of us were arrested that night.

In high school, I had always been the guy to keep my friends out of trouble with the police. They'd tell their buddies, "Y'all need to take a listen from Ronnie on how to talk with the police." But that night, after I had broken the law, I didn't show those police officers respect. When they arrested me, I deserved it. They were just doing their job and upholding the law. We were released on bail and sent back to base with a court date.

As is customary with the Marines, any time you get in trouble off the base, they send someone with you to your court date so they can give a report back to base if you get detained. Luckily, Sgt. Sloan got the job of being our escort. He was always a lot of fun. We went to a fast-food restaurant and joked around while eating steak biscuits. An older gentleman, seated at a table across from us, decided to join in our conversation. He was quite the jokester and fit right in.

Later on, we showed up at the courthouse and joined the others sitting in the courtroom. We were all eyes on the door behind the judge's desk, and when it finally opened, out came the same man we had been joking with at the restaurant. Surely we couldn't be that lucky, but we were! When it came our turn to stand before him, the judge said, "Didn't I just have a biscuit with you boys?"

Wearing the biggest smiles we could muster, we all said, "Yes, sir!"

The charge against us was defrauding an innkeeper, and the young waitress who had served us our meals was there. But somehow, the judge seemed to think that the waitress was at fault in a completely different matter involving a woman and three Marines in a hotel room. So, after the judge scolded us for getting into trouble ("You boys should have known better, being Marines"), he lit into that waitress for inappropriate behavior.

It was all my buddies and I could do not to bust out laughing as that poor waitress, shocked by the judge's innuendo and misunderstanding, endured his fatherly lecture on the proper conduct of a young lady.

"As for you three Marines," he said, "you are fined the amount specified and time served. Case closed," and he slammed his gavel.

My binge drinking was getting out of control, and it finally landed me in some serious trouble. After a long weekend of drinking in town, my buddy Steve and I decided to head back to base that Sunday night and finish off the weekend drinking at the E Club. We heard, "last call for alcohol," just as the officer of the day came in with his driver and ordered everybody to drink up and get out.

Steve and I downed our beers and left. It was raining outside and a long walk back to the barracks. Steve looked at me with a big smile and said, "Don't you have a jeep license?"

"Yeah." As a com-radio operator, I had a license to drive jeeps with radio equipment.

Drunker than Cooter Brown, Steve and I jumped into the officer of the day's jeep and found the keys still in the ignition. So I cranked the jeep, and we took off just as the officer of the day and his driver came running out, hollering for us to stop. But we flipped them the bird and kept driving, laughing as we sped away.

Alcohol makes you do things that you would never think of doing while sober, so instead of parking the jeep and running, we decided to go mudding. We were having a great time, too, until we got the jeep stuck in some old tank tracks.

That's when we started to sober up. To cover our fingerprints, we wiped the rest of the jeep down with mud and beat it back to our barracks.

Since we were also covered with mud, I thought we should stay out of sight, and walk further down the wood line, but Steve wanted to go a different way, so we did—another mistake. By the barracks, we saw an MP, so we started up the nearest set of stairs to make him think we were going to our room.

He shouted for us to stop, but we kept climbing stairs until we heard him lock and load his weapon. Then we both froze and turned around with our hands up over our heads.

"Why are you stopping us?" Steve asked, playing dumb.

"We're looking for two male Caucasians, and you guys fit the description."

"Well it can't be us," I said, pointing to Steve. "He's an Indian," and we busted up laughing. It was true, Steve was full-blooded Apache, but the MP was not amused. He called in more MPs, and they took us to our barracks and told us not to leave our room until they sent for us the next morning, which by that time was only an hour away.

At the Naval Criminal Investigative Service, MPs marched us down a long hallway interrupted every so often with a set of metal doors. Each time one of those heavy doors slammed shut behind me, I sobered up a little more. They put Steve and me into different rooms, alone, and left us there for a while. I was a mess—tired, hung over, and this time in serious trouble. I bowed my head and said, "God, I need You. Please help me."

Later, with a bright light in my face, three officers started grilling me with questions. Steve and I had agreed to stick with our "not guilty" story, and I did until one of the officers told me the charge was enough to send me to Leavenworth—a place that will put the fear of God into the hardest Marine.

"If you confess," one interrogator said, "the charges of unauthorized joy riding will be dropped, and your battalion commander along with Capt. Klotz will decide what happens next." My battalion commander, Lt. Col. Beavers, had always liked me. He knew that I was good at my job and that my drinking was getting the best of me. I decided to confess and take my chances with him deciding my fate. And boy, he must have liked me because Lt. Col. Beavers (and Capt. Klotz) saved my hide. Even though I lost my rank and suffered some severe punishment—breaking rocks at the Correctional Custody Unit—it was still better than what could have happened to me.

I felt very blessed to have had Lt. Col. Beavers on my side. He saw that I was a good Marine, just one who was on a self-destructive course and needed help getting his head on straight. I guess God sent me a coach in the Corps after all. I just wish I had realized it sooner.

Still, despite all the trouble I'd been in, I was determined to push through and be a good Marine.

My first test came when I was sent back to Marine Corps Air Ground Combat Center in Twentynine Palms with my communications unit, along with other units from the 2nd Marine Division Camp Lejeune. More Marines from 1st Marine Division Camp Pendleton joined us there to take part in their combined arms exercises (also known as "war games") on the installation's nine hundred square miles of desert.[3]

These joint exercises were taken very seriously by the brass and involved a lot of coordination down through the ranks. A buddy of mine let me know that during a meeting concerning our unit, one of the sergeants told Sgt. Sloan (one of the two sergeants over my group) that since I seemed to be a troublemaker, he would make sure that I was assigned the worst jeep that he could find to drive during the exercises.

"But Sloan stood up for you, man," my buddy said. "He said you may have gotten into some trouble, but you'd be one of the best, if not *the* best, com man he would have during these war games."

Sgt. Sloan's confidence in me meant a lot, and I wasn't about to let him down. When our first assignments were issued, the sergeant who had promised to get me the worst com jeep he could find stayed true to his word—my jeep barely stayed running. To top it off, he put me at end of the convoy. Along with all of the other com man duties assigned to me, I had to keep shifting gears and popping the clutch to keep that jeep moving through all that high desert terrain.

It was a true test of all the training I'd received—the closest simulation to real war that I would experience during my enlistment, and just to be part of it was amazing. I got to see, close up, the capabilities and readiness of the United States Marine Corps, each unit working in precision, and it was awesome.

Artillery would pound the mountains, then I would hear the call over my radio to cease fire, and a second later the Marine air wing would streak by and bomb the same area. Then the tanks rolled in, firing away as the infantry began to advance forward. It was an impressive display of military power, and it made me proud to be part of such an amazing fighting force.

Back at our main camp — A-frame huts made of plywood — the sergeant from California asked the major if he was happy with his driver who was also his com man.

"Yes, but I want to make a change," he said. "When we go back out, I want the Marine from the end of the convoy to be my driver and radio man." When the sergeant asked why, the major said, "I watched that Marine while we were out this week. I saw how he got the worst jeep to drive and the worst assignments, but he never complained and always did his job. I want that Marine working for me."

The next time we went out, I drove the major in a brand-spanking-new Humvee and ended up doing recon for the whole unit. Every so often, we would drive by that sergeant who had tried to make my life miserable, and I just smiled. I wanted him and everyone else to know that while I did have some personal issues to work through, I was still a good Marine, I was still a proud Marine, and I was good at the job they had given me to do.

I spent the rest of my service time at Camp Lejeune. In fact, I turned twenty-one on the demolition range. I told my gunny, "If you get me blown up on my twenty-first birthday, I'll haunt you forever."

Demolition seemed to be a fitting place to start my last months in the Marine Corps because I felt like I was self-destructing. My drinking, running from God, and worry over things at home were taking a toll. Here I was, a grown man, but I still worried about my momma. She and Danny had decided to divorce, and I hated that she was on her own, unhappy, and me not there to help. As long as I could remember, my job, at least the way I saw it, had always been to protect her.

When I was eight, I remember the local news reporting that a female apartment manager had been abducted from her office and was missing. At that time, Momma had a similar job, and I was terrified that somebody evil would take her. I loved my momma and felt it was up to me to keep her safe. Usually, this amounted to me throwing ugly looks at any man who dared to look her way (Momma was a beautiful woman). But the threat of abduction called for military tactics.

I dug out the army equipment that our neighbor, Jet Rainer, had given me when he got out—an old helmet, canvas belt, canteen, and ammo holder. With my gear strapped on and BB gun in hand, I hid in the bushes outside Momma's office, keeping guard. She had no idea what I was doing until a "very suspicious" man showed up at her office. When he went through the door, I repositioned under her office window. As Momma went over the details of apartment amenities, I raised up real slow to see through her window. She happened to glance my way long enough to notice my furrowed brow, and when our eyes met, I'll never forget the shocked look on her face.

After the man left, she called me out of the bushes and looked me up and down in my full combat dress. Momma smiled and said, "Son, thank you for loving me and wanting to protect me, but it's not needed. I'm fine. Now go play with your friends." She thought that's what I did, but I just moved my surveillance to a nearby location and kept an eye on her for days.

Besides not being there for Momma during her divorce, I also knew I caused her worry. Even though it was peacetime, she was afraid I would get sent off to war. What helped her, she later told me, was a lady at church who asked, "You've been praying for Ronnie?" Momma nodded. She took Momma's hand and pointed to the center of her palm and said, "There. That's where God has Ronnie, in the palm of His hand." The only war I was engaged in was a spiritual one. At every turn, it seemed, I was reminded of the call God had on my life.

I remember being in my barracks one time, and we had a new roommate who had only been there a week or two. It was a Friday — payday — and I was getting dressed to go out. I had put on my jeans and my cowboy boots, and, as I was buttoning my shirt, this new guy says, "You know who you remind me of?"

"No, who?" In my mind I was thinking, *John Wayne.*

He said, "Man, you remind me of a preacher."

I wanted to knock him out, but he didn't know that he'd hit a raw nerve — I didn't even want to look like a preacher let alone be one. In fact, avoiding ministry was the only real goal I had for my return to civilian life, which was now within spitting distance.

On my last day in the Marine Corps, my gunny sergeant came to the barracks to say goodbye, and that meant a lot to me. It also gave me the chance to ask him something that had bothered me from the start of my service.

"I volunteered for every deployment offered," I said, "but you never let me go. Why?"

Gunny grinned and said, "Well, I only had two guys that I knew I could count on to do their jobs, and you were one of them. So I kept you here and sent the others away to get them out of my hair."

I laughed with him, but I was still disappointed that I never got to deploy or defend America on foreign soil. Little did I know that one day I would get the opportunity to fight for freedom right here at home, on a football field.

I was in the middle of that fight when my son Chase asked me privately how CJ, who had been his friend and close to our family, could protest during the anthem and then be so ugly about me on social media.

I said, "Sometimes we turn on the very people who care about us the most," and when I said that, the faces of two Marines who had stuck their necks out for me years ago came to mind.

I told Chase about some of my troubles in the Marines, and how Lt. Col. Beavers and Capt. Klotz had defended me to their superiors and helped me, but at the time, I didn't appreciate it.

"Lt. Col. Beavers once asked me if I thought Capt. Klotz had my back and I said, 'No, sir.' To this day, that answer haunts me. I would give anything to go back and change what I said to a 'Yes, sir.' And if I ever find those two men, I will go to them face-to-face and apologize for being so stupid and not recognizing just how much each one did for me. The thing is, son, when you're young and bull-headed, you make mistakes, and when you get older, you wish you could go back and undo them. To have to live with knowing that you disrespected someone who actually cared about you is a lifelong sentence of regret. I learned that lesson the hard way."

CHAPTER 11

THE FALLOUT

~——,

My time in the Marine Corps has always been a measuring stick in my life. Whenever I came up against a tough situation, I'd think, *This can't be any worse than boot camp.* But the onslaught of hate I received after cutting CJ and Larry from the Sharks was worse. And unlike thirteen weeks of boot camp, this was several months of pure hell. After that game, after the initial story broke and Larry went on TV and said that I'd made him and CJ "script [*sic*] down in our uniform—pads, the pants, and all in front of everyone," I was bombarded by every liberal media out there. They wanted to show the nation who this racist coach was who publicly "humiliated" these young men after he had kicked them off of his football team.

The way most media operate today, reporters no longer investigate a story to get both sides because their networks are only interested in presenting one. They lure the public into the arena of national debate with click-bait headlines like Larry's quote and the argument of refusing a teen's right to protest. Afterward, they call a guy like me into the center of that arena, gagged and blindfolded, to be judged by the haters and the half-informed who take aim and fire incriminating posts and Tweets at will.

At least that's how it worked in my case. On Facebook and Twitter, people viciously attacked my Christianity, my church, and me. I received several death threats, and since local news crews had done me the favor of broadcasting images of my church and our football field—the same property my home sits on—it was especially concerning to read on Messenger, "I know where you live, and we're gonna have fun with you."

I deleted all of the threats because I didn't want my wife or kids seeing them, but sitting in my chair late at night while they slept, I scrolled through them again in my mind. When you're threatened like that, you can't help but react. I told my kids, "Make sure you don't wear anything with our Sharks logo on it to school or at work. I don't want anybody making you a target over this. And when you leave the house for any reason, make sure to lock the deadbolt." The look on their faces made my heart ache. I had spent my entire adult life keeping my family safe, and now, because of a decision I had made, they were all in danger. That feeling alone nearly broke me.

Added to my worry for Stacey and the kids was concern for my church. What had taken Stacey and me fourteen years to build was smeared in seconds by people who hate. Comments on our Victory & Praise Worship Center Facebook page[1] read like a shootout between the haters and my supporters:

"Christians don't put other people down. You lift them up and support them. This must be a satanic Church."

"This place supports racism and bigotry! You should never worship at this place!!"

"A disgusting bunch of Anti-American racist bigots. Civil Liberties aren't welcome here. An embarrassing disgrace to Christianity."

> *"Thank You Coach Mitchem for your hard work and dedication to God and our football program. We stand behind you 100%. You are a GOD fearing Man. I appreciate All you do. . . . #Sharks#finsup"*

> *"Much love for Pastor Ronnie, all who know him personally, know his love for God, for this country, and for people of all backgrounds. He's a man of character and respect. A man who stands for truth without compromise. Love you brother!"*

"Pure racist. . . . I pray black people stay away from this place. . . . It's ran by the kkk."

"You should stay clear of a church that has a Pastor that is clearly a White Supremacist and suppresses the constitutional rights of its members/players."

"Racist pastor. Should not be allowed to preach. Enough said."

"We love and support you Brother Ronnie. Stand on the word of GOD."

"Shame for teaching your hate rules over the horrible ways blacks are treated in this nation and taking right away from others as bad Christians ALWAYS do. We need to take away your tax-exempt status and pick your school. I call on all people of color to protest this school that cares more about a veteran racist coach then students they teach. BTW this is not over we will remember this when all GOP haters are voted out of office. You are on the wrong side of history."

"This Mitchem joker should be fired! What sort of so-called christian cannot forgive such a mild transgression. Keep your kids away from this freak!"

*"Appreciate you Brother Ronnie
Mitchem for taking that right stand!
I've been to your church and I know you
all preach the truth. We are praying for
you Pastor Ronnie! The Lord is with
you, and your family!!"*

"Led by a white supremacist. His black student's issues are secondary to him. He endan-
gers them by posting their image on his FB
to be antagonised by his white supremacist
friends. In turn he gets to exalt himself in the
eyes of his white supremacist friends."

"Did it excite you to make those kids strip on
the field you pedophile POS!"

*Great man! Great patriot! Thank you for
your service and for standing up for our
country. Without people respecting our
country, we will soon have no country.*

"Giving a piece of cloth so much power and
respect is the same thing as idolatry. And you
are a pastor who preaches the word of God. How
can this piece of cloth do anything for anyone?
When you served the country (not the flag) you
were fighting to protect the rights of freedom
of speech and expression. I am sure you don't

agree with a lot of things your partitioners [sic; parishioners] do, but do you strip them down and humiliate them in front of others? Or did you do it because they were children of color? Maybe you should pray and ask God to guide you on this one sir. I'm sure he would tell you not to put so much emphasis, hope, pride and faith in a piece of cloth. The flag nor the anthem does anything for the American people. It's how we work together, pray together, love one another and accept each other's differences that makes us special. Not the flag!"

"Don't go!! Pastor here is a covert racist, not a save space for people of color or children. Had teens strip in front of him for his viewing pleasure."

"No chance this is a good place to worship, unless you're praying to a wolf in sheep's clothing. When you don't put God first, there is no way you can profess to be a minster of the church. This is church and 'paster/coach' is a total scam. WWJD??"

> *"Thank you, Pastor Ronnie Mitchum for standing for our Lord and for standing for our Flag and Anthem. God Bless you and yours. Stand strong, we are standing with you."*

"In 2015, I shared the following with Coach Mitchem. I spent a lot of time with and around Coach Mitchem and this was, and still is, based on observation. 'I really enjoy football, but your program is about far more than football. You are helping build young men with good integrity and great character. In today's world, more and more people are moving away from raising children with any values at all. The fact that you take on the task to instill true honest values in young men is a blessing.'"

"There is nothing Christian about this uneducated, racist 'pastor' who thinks he knows best. Stay away. He is full of hate and pride, yet is illiterate himself. Nothing Christlike about this place."

"When fascism comes to America it will be wrapped in the flag and carrying a cross."

One commenter included a picture of people making the Hitler salute and wrote, "I also find it hilariously ironic how your FB pages banner is of people holding up their arms in a slant. Kind of familiar if you ask me." The reference was to people in our church lifting their hands in praise and worship of the Lord. That same person wanted me fired, as so many others demanded because the news also failed to report that I was a volunteer and unassociated with any school organization.

Another commenter erroneously referred to my Coach of the Week award from the Houston Texans Foundation and Houston Methodist before adding a bold-faced lie: "Texans just cut a $2500 check to a man who made 2 black kids strip off their uniforms for kneeling against racism & police brutality, sells white supremacist gear, is a Trump supporter & is boycotting the NFL. Sounds about White." The only things we sell in our church are Christian teaching materials, gospel music, and Shark t-shirts.

It wasn't enough to assassinate my character. It was as if their outbursts were designed to trigger more left-wing activism from Black Lives Matter or antifa, so they would join in the attack against me, my family, and my church. I don't think most people realize how nasty the left really is. They hurl judgment without knowing or caring about the facts. None of my new enemies had ever set foot in my church or heard me preach, yet they wanted me to burn, as one lady wrote, "in the hottest part of hell."

I tried to let all of the ugly comments roll off, and there were thousands, most so foul and vulgar that I refused to repeat them here. But the truth is, they stung. The ones that hurt most condemned me for missing the opportunity to use this protest as a "teachable moment," and that I was an overall bad influence on the boys. I knew that wasn't true because I'd heard just the opposite from so many of my players and their parents from past and present seasons.

And they didn't just tell me how much my football program meant to them, they showed me. On that first Sunday
morning after the protest, a bunch of them showed up at
church wearing their Sharks jerseys. Later, several players
came to me, individually, to thank me and offer their support.

The day after my October 3 interview with Frances
Swaggart on SBN, I went to the mailbox and noticed a
couple of letters. I looked at the return addresses and said
to Stacey, "I'm getting mail from people I don't know." The
next day, a small stack of letters came in from more people
thanking me for my stand. Conservatives, I learned, still take
the time to handwrite letters, use clean language, and sign
their real names.

Many wrote their notes of encouragement on patriotic
stationery, so under images of Old Glory I read notes like
this one: "When I heard about your players being taken out
of a football game AND off the team because of their stance
about THEIR flag, I spiritedly said out loud, 'Good for that
coach,' for as an adult who works with youth daily, if YOU
don't show them what character means, they certainly can't
learn it from their peers or even some other adult because
YOU may be the ONLY positive reinforcement in their lives."

One card I received was from a church thanking me for
taking a stand, and it looked to me as if every person in the
congregation had signed it. Others texted or posted their
support, and I even received a few positive phone calls.

One morning I answered the church phone and a very
polite lady asked, "May I please speak to your football coach
or athletic director?"

"Yes, ma'am," I said, smiling to myself as I mentally switched hats from pastor to athletic director. "This is he."

"Well, I don't have a son who plays football," she said, "but a kid in my church played against your football team, and he came to church, and all he could talk about was how awesome your team was because the guys were so classy and Christlike. He said he'd never played a team like that, and I just want you to know that whatever you're doing, keep doing it."

I was also honored to receive from the National Memorial Ladies and the Fallen Warriors Memorial a US flag that was flown over the Fallen Warriors Memorial and had also withstood the ravages of Hurricane Harvey. They presented it saying, "To you, Coach, for your selfless service as a Marine and for your devotion to our flag. Thank you for honoring and teaching our youth about sacrifices and respect of our great flag."

While Stacey and I deeply appreciated the support of all those who reached out to us, hearing from veterans was especially meaningful to me.

There was the pilot from 101st Airborne Division, who served in Vietnam. In bold black marker he wrote, "Great decision, Coach! When the anthem plays, we stand at attention with hand over heart! God bless you and God bless America! Semper Fi!"

I also received a phone call from a Silver Star recipient who lives in Fort Worth. He was a corpsman in the Navy — a conscientious objector who refused to shoot a gun but saved several men in Vietnam. "I appreciate your stand for

America," he said. "That kneeling stuff is disgraceful. It's high time somebody had the backbone to stand up to this act of disrespect. Thank you."

His words left me speechless. I felt totally unworthy to be thanked like that by an America hero.

Within a couple of days, we had heard from supporters all over America, Austria, Germany, India, Europe, and I even had word sent to me from Marines serving in a combat zone.

Momma had come for a visit, and she was blown away by all the letters of support. "Oh my Lord," she said, "I can't believe you're getting all this mail." She and I did our best to respond to every letter I received. But my biggest encouragers were Stacey and the kids. Even though all of this caused them a lot of worry and heartache, they never once wavered in their support for me or my decision. They seemed to know just when I needed a hug or a word of encouragement.

Away from home, when I went out to run my usual errands, I was on high alert. If people looked at me, I couldn't help but wonder if they recognized me from the news, and if so, were they haters or supporters? One minute I was reading a Post-It Note stuck on my car windshield that said, "What other guaranteed constitutional rights do you want to suspend? You'd make a good Nazi! Christ weeps at your narrow mindedness," and the next, someone was shaking my hand, thanking me.

At the dry cleaners, while picking up my suit for Sunday, the owner came out to greet me. I had no idea that he even knew who I was, but he stretched out his hand to shake mine and said, "I agree with you and what you did. These kneelers need to go to another country and find out how good they have it in America." This man was from another country, so I felt that he understood firsthand just how blessed we are to be Americans. Unfortunately, many who are born here do not.

Yet even with all of the encouraging support, the public backlash from the media's misreporting still hovered over our lives, the same way Hurricane Harvey had settled over Houston until families were forced to evacuate. All of the ugly things being said about me took a huge toll on my family. Stacey and the kids were constantly worried that something would happen to me. Every time I left the house, Stacey asked, "Got your gun with you?" and I always did.

I didn't realize how worried Stacey really was until she collapsed one day at home. She and I were discussing the situation, and she got up to go into the kitchen for some water when suddenly she fell forward, face first, onto the floor. I jumped out of my chair and went to her. I propped her up, made sure she was breathing okay, and held her. She came to fairly quickly, but in all of our years of marriage, I'd never seen my wife faint before. When she fell, it was like my heart hit the ground with her.

"God," I prayed, "why is all of this happening?" I didn't understand how our whole world could be caving in over this. What was wrong with people? Had the world gone mad? We went from cheering our team on a Friday night to having to defend ourselves simply for loving our country, all because two boys wanted a few minutes of fame. I could handle the hate and the pressure, but seeing how it was affecting my family took it to a whole new level.

Another big concern was the safety of my football team. Parents and players were calling me and asking if Monday's football practice was still on. They too, had been following the news and the hateful comments on social media. In all my years of playing and coaching football, I never thought I'd hear the question, "Is it safe to come to practice?" Thankfully, one of my assistant coaches is a retired police officer, and I made sure he was able to be at all of our practices. (By the way, none of my players—including Larry and CJ—ever had a problem with this coach, or he with them).

For home games, we hired a security officer, only we didn't play on our own field, the Shark Tank. Before the football season had even started, and without knowing that any of this would happen, I'd made arrangements for us to play our home games on a field ninety minutes away. This worked out well as the field was fenced with only one entrance, so it was easier to secure, plus it was far enough away that the lazy media left us alone.

We were distracted though. At practice, every time an unfamiliar car pulled up near the field, we all stopped to see who it was. Morale was sinking; the team had lost some of its fire. And, for the first time in my coaching career, the joy of coaching football had slipped away. I was ready for the season to end, and after a few more games, my players picked up on it. During a time out at one of our games, Chase said, "Dad, you've got to believe in us."

I realized then that I would never be the same coach or the same man again. It felt as though my heart and part of my soul had been ripped out, and I was struggling under the heavy load of worry and stress. I never felt lonelier.

At church, to keep the congregation safe, we hired security for our services in case we were attacked. If anyone thought this was an overreaction on my part, I'm sure they changed their minds after someone shot out our church sign one night. We trusted God to protect us, and part of that protection included our church members who were former military — Army, Navy, Air Force, and Marines — along with others who owned conceal-and-carry permits. These parishioners became part of our new security force. Again, if anyone thought this was overkill, they didn't think it for long.

On November 5, Devin Patrick Kelley walked into a church two hundred miles from mine and shot twenty-six people to death. He injured twenty more, some critically. There may have been more casualties had an armed citizen not acted and shot Kelley, slowing him considerably as he left the church and climbed into his vehicle. Kelley, too, died that day.[2]

This horrible tragedy raised a national question, "Should pastors be armed?" My answer to that is yes. As a man, former Marine, pastor, and coach, I feel it's my duty to protect what God has put in my charge, and that includes my family, my congregation, and my players. Like many believers across the country, the mass shooting at the First Baptist Church in Sutherland Springs made us at Victory & Praise realize that we could no longer take the simple act of worshipping God safely for granted, and I believe that united us more as a church family. Together we learned again the American lesson: when freedom is threatened, you must fight all the more to protect it.

CHAPTER 12

REPENTANCE

⟶

As a boy, I believed. It's easier then, when you're small and God is big. Just look into the eyes of any toddler riding high on the muscled shoulder of his dad, and you'll see childlike faith in full bloom. From then on, whatever a father says about a son to that boy, it's gospel. My dad didn't say much to me or about me until the end of his life. Before that, he was mostly someone who sat on the bench in my heart, unable to play in the game.

Nearly everything I learned about being a man I collected from others: how to shake a man's hand firmly and look him in the eye — that was from my stepdad, Danny. How to see a job through — Coach Ward taught me that one on the field. Respect for my country I learned mostly from Marines.

But how to fight is something I picked up on my own. I'm not talking about physical fights — those were never a problem — but fighting for myself, for my dreams, that's where I fell short.

More than anything, I wanted to play college football, and in high school, that dream was within reach. When I was still in tenth grade, Evangel College offered me a football scholar-ship, which back then was unheard of. After seeing me play, their head coach came to talk to me. "When you graduate high school," he said, "we'll have a scholarship waiting for you. All you have to do is let me know, and you're coming to Evangel."

That same year, I played in an all-star game where I missed, by only five points, the most valuable player award, which came with a full ride scholarship to Mississippi State. The player I lost to was a senior who turned heads when, in one play, he intercepted the ball and sealed the game.

My junior year, when the football program at Bell Road ended, I transferred during Christmas break to Robert E. Lee High School. Lee played in the highest division in the state of Alabama. I went out for spring training and won a starting offensive guard position. My goal was to play defense, but I was willing to take what I could get.

At practice, the coaches had us doing drills, going against the strongest guy on the team. He wasn't the biggest, but he was the strongest—a monster—and I blew right by him when nobody else could. The defensive coach said, "Do that again," and I blew by him a second time. After that, they put me on defense.

So there I was, in the biggest division in the state of Alabama already with two starting positions. The rest of the team, all buddies it seemed to me, didn't like the idea of a new guy, especially one from a Christian school, taking positions away from some of their friends. And they weren't exactly congratulating me on the scholarship offer they knew I had from Evangel.

I got along with everybody, but I never really felt a part of that team, and the coaches knew it. Their solution was to hold me back a year with the promise of a scholarship to the school of my choosing. "He's that good of a football player," they told Momma. "But we need him to get his grades up." They wanted me on the team they were building for the following year, a guarantee you could say, that they'd take the state championship. But when I told my friends, they laughed it off. My buddy Blake pulled me aside and said, "All of us are graduating next year, Ron. Gonna get kinda lonely around here, don't you think?"

The biggest decision of my young life was in front of me, but did I pray about it? No. God and I had grown apart. I didn't talk it over with anyone. I just one day decided that I didn't want to do it. I told myself it was because I couldn't take another year of homework and studying and tests, which was partly true. I had no problem applying myself on the field, but pushing myself in the classroom was difficult.

But that wasn't the whole truth. Deep down, there was a little boy who needed his father to steady him and say, "You can do this, son." But I wasn't going to hear those words, not from my dad and not from God. In that silence, my heart grew steadily colder toward both of them. So when the coaches asked for my decision, I didn't fight for that football scholarship the way I wish to God I would have. Had I stayed, I would have been on Lee's team when the Generals won the state title the next year, and I would have gone on to play in college, tuition-free.

Instead, I let go of my dream with both hands, and walked out into life. I changed high schools again, played more football, and joined the Marines through the delayed entry program. Before I knew it, my senior year was over, and I graduated from Landmark High School, feeling lost and alone. I needed to find out what I was really made of, and I figured the Marines would show me — and they did. After they knocked me down to nothing, they built me back up into feeling like something.

But after three years in the Corps, I had to change out of that uniform and military life and figure out what was next. I stumbled through odd jobs in construction and worked for a while as a butcher in a grocery store before heading to Troy, Alabama to drive a truck. When you're running from God, there's no better place to be than behind the wheel of a semi. I traveled coast-to-coast, logging thousands of miles, yet I had no clue where I was going in life. I'd drive and think and drive and think, and my thoughts always turned back to the Lord. I'd look out at the beautiful scenery — the Rockies in Colorado, the Pacific in California, the desert in Arizona — and be suddenly overcome with appreciation for God's creation. Or a gospel song would come on the radio and snap me back to times when I had clapped along with that same hymn, happy and full of joy. And then there was Momma. I'd call from the road to check on her and feel my throat tighten when she'd say, "I'm praying for you, Ronnie," and I knew that she was.

On one of those calls, Momma reminded me of a time when I felt I'd done something horrible. I was a teenager, new at driving, and I'd stopped at the local station to pump some gas. I was in a hurry, and when I finished with the gas, I drove off without paying. When I realized what I'd done, I was embarrassed and didn't know what to do. Momma said, "Just go down there and tell the clerk what happened. Tell her you're sorry, and pay what you owe." I asked Momma if she'd come along, but she wouldn't. "You made the mistake; you fix it," she said. When I finally got the nerve to go there and tell what happened, the clerk lady smiled and said, "Ronnie, I didn't have any worries about you. I knew you'd come back with the money."

I was in a far worse fix now, and I couldn't bring myself to tell Momma that I was struggling with my faith. But Momma knew. "You're going to sway, Ronnie. But you're going to come back to God," she said. The truth was, I had tried to come back. More than once I had come to that place of brokenness where I flat-out bawled and told God how much I needed Him. Things would go okay for a while, but as soon as I slipped — and I always did — I'd let go.

I was a grown man who couldn't find his childlike faith. After several fits and starts with God, I decided that since I couldn't live a perfect life, there was no need to keep trying. I didn't want to be a hypocrite, so I gave up on Christianity and went back to living my life the way that I wanted to live it. That's about the time I got a phone call, saying my dad was really sick and I needed to come see him. Just a few months earlier, I had spent a little time with him, and he was fine. Now he wasn't. His liver was tired of all the drinking, and his mind was tortured from years of guilt and hate.

At the hospital, I looked at my dad, forty-three years old and dying, and I struggled with how to feel. He was my father, but I didn't know him. If he was still angry at life, I didn't know it. If he had made his peace with God, I didn't know that, either. I only knew that heaven and hell were real places, and his time for choosing was hours away. I stepped out of his hospital room, and just like that, Dad left me again without telling me where he was going.

It was my fault that I didn't know; I should have made sure Dad was saved. Why didn't I pray for him when I had the chance? "God, I need You," I prayed, and then turned from Him to a wall and leaned there.

With a new drive to make something of myself, I started up my own carpet cleaning business out of the back of my Chevy. Soon I had several contracts, my own van, and a reputation for doing a good, professional job. On the side, I reached for a new goal — to be a football coach — and I enrolled in college part-time to earn my degree. Between work and school I was busy, but I still found time to spend my hard-earned money with friends at the local bar.

I still prayed, on occasion — petitions that had dwindled to requests such as, "Lord help me not to go to the bar tonight." But my desire to drink was stronger, and I'd end up on a barstool with my buddies. The bartender and I had a running joke: I'd ask for another drink, and he'd say, "I thought you were only having two," and I'd come back with,

"I meant two, too many." Around 2 a.m., I'd stumble home drunk, flip on Christian television, and hear a song or a testimony that would make me miss God.

Nearly every night after work, I'd sit on that barstool for hours, listening in on slurred conversations about how horrible life was. I heard sad stories told by people who had probably never known true happiness. That's where my misery came in. I knew better. In my heart I knew that true happiness could only come through knowing Jesus Christ and serving Him. But I had traded all that to sit here with these drunks, numbing the pain.

If one of them had sat down on the barstool next to mine and asked about my life, I would have said, "I'm more miserable than all of you because I'm running from God, which is stupid because you can't outrun God. No matter what I do, no matter where I go, I can't get away from Him. He's called me into the ministry, but I don't want to go. You know what that's like? It means I toss and turn in my bed at night because that's when He deals with my heart. He wants me to give up all of this — my drinking, my partying, and my good-paying job — and follow Him into ministry when everybody knows that preachers are poor as dirt. Sometimes I get so mad that I holler at Him to leave me alone. I say, 'Go find somebody else to preach Your Word!' Don't get me wrong, I don't hate God; I just don't want the load of other people's souls on my shoulders."

The bar buddy I wanted most to hear all of this was my dad. I found myself missing him more, and somehow drinking made me feel closer and more compassionate to who he was. With a mug of beer in my hand, I could accept him. I'd always told myself that I never wanted to be like him, but here I was, learning his ways. It was a time when I didn't want to be good, but I couldn't be bad. I was a son who had to choose which father to follow: Dad or God. I wanted Dad, but he was gone.

To my friends, I was a success. Only twenty-five years old and the owner of my own business with my eye set on coaching football, I was playing hard between the whistles, but somehow still losing the big game. I decided to let God back in, but on my terms.

"Lord, I want You in my life again," I prayed. "Please help me."

I stopped going to the bar, cut the parties, and found a nearby church to attend. In a bargain with God, I reached out to Evangel College, the school that had offered me a football scholarship, to see if I could complete my degree in physical education with a minor in Bible studies. If that worked, my plan was to graduate, coach football during the week, and preach on weekends. It sounded like a fair deal to me.

When I called Evangel's athletic department, I found myself talking to the same head coach who had offered me the scholarship in high school. He remembered me and said, "If you're half the football player you were back then, I'll give you a half scholarship to come and *play*." This shocked me. I hadn't played football for years. I was getting a second shot at my dream, and this time, I was going for it. I sold my carpet cleaning business and anything else I couldn't fit into my Ford F-150. Before making the trip from Florida to Springfield, Missouri, I decided to drive an hour north and see Momma. She had since gotten remarried to her high school sweetheart, Steve Brown, and I couldn't have been happier for both of them. Steve was the great love of my momma's life, and they had planned to marry back then, but his father forbade it. Momma and Steve were forced to part ways, and the separation devastated her. It was during this low point in her life that she started dating Bo Mitchem—my dad.

When I got to Momma's house, she and Steve were packing, getting ready to leave for vacation, but she still found time to cook me up a big dinner—fried pork chops, squash, peas, fried okra, and hot cornbread. Man, can my momma cook. She was happy for me but concerned that I'd made the decision to move so quickly.

"Are you sure about this, Ronnie?"

"Momma, they're giving me a chance to *play* again. At my age, that's a miracle. And I'll be working toward my degree. It's the chance of a lifetime."

"It all sounds good, son. I just want God's best for you."

We said our goodbyes, and Momma and Steve left for vacation. I had the house all to myself to rest up before my own trip the next day. I finished off the rest of Momma's good cooking and fell off to sleep on the couch.

Later that night I woke up, suddenly, and felt the presence of God all around me. It was so strong that I was afraid to look up. No longer was Jesus just a person I'd been ignoring and putting off or a power source that I occasionally tapped into to whenever I was stranded in life. No, at that moment, the one who had saved me with His own precious blood was standing in that living room, and He knew me. He knew everything about me, and yet He still loved me with a love that I still don't fully understand.

I felt like Peter must have felt after he had denied the Lord. Peter, who had walked on the water toward Christ, seen Him perform miracle after miracle, ate with Him, and confessed to Him that He was the Christ. Like Peter, I had walked with the Lord and seen Him save people after I'd stepped out in faith and shared my testimony with them—each salvation a miracle. And, like Peter, I had denied knowing Jesus. Every time I stepped away from Him and toward sin, toward my own ambitions, I had denied Him. Now, like the great fisherman, I, too, was hearing the cock crow and seeing, in my spirit, the Lord looking upon me.

On my knees, I broke. Weeping the bitter tears of true repentance, I prayed from my heart, "God, please forgive me for running from You and for all of my sin. Please come into my heart and be my Lord and my Savior. I'm so sorry for everything I've done. I love You, Jesus, and I need You to wash me in Your blood and change my life. Father, if You will have me, I want to come home. I want to be the man that You want me to be—a man after Your own heart."

I hardly had the last word out of my mouth before I heard the Lord respond to my heart, "Son, you left me, but I never left you, and I never will. My door always was and always is open to you."

With the joy of my salvation restored, I lifted my hands and praised the Lord. I worshipped Him for being a merciful and loving God and for loving me even though I found it hard to love myself. I stepped outside and stood next to my truck, packed with everything I owned, and looked up at the moon, full and bright. I couldn't wait for morning to break and see where the Lord would lead me.

When I got to Evangel College, the National Association of Intercollegiate Athletics informed me that I was one credit short, which made me ineligible to play in the coming football season. I prayed about it and felt that God was telling me to stop my pursuit of coaching and focus instead on full-time ministry. That was hard to hear, especially after seeing the college's football field — the first field I'd walked on in more than six years. Only God knows how much I wanted to play again, and, if I couldn't play, at least coach. But God doesn't bargain. He wanted me in full-time ministry.

I transferred to Central Bible College, which is also in Springfield and associated with the Assemblies of God. After a short time there, I felt led to go back home and start preaching, which I did at my Uncle Bill Locke's church. Soon after that, I was pastoring a church of my own.

Those first sermons of mine were short but passionate. I could feel the anointing of the Holy Spirit on me, especially as I made the altar call. Not one of those went by without my thinking of Dad. People would come to the altar and kneel down, and I'd think of Dad in that hospital bed. When he knew I was there, his open eyes had flickered.

At times, guilt over not praying for him could still overwhelm me, and I'd pray for God to give me peace about it. During one of those prayers, the Lord spoke to my heart and said, "Don't blame yourself for your dad's decisions. Your grandmother raised him in church, and there were other times when I offered him the opportunity to be saved."

Some time later, one of my relatives told me, "You know, when your dad found out that you were thinking about being a minister he said, 'I'm proud of my boy. He's gone to get his life straightened out. He's going to be a preacher.'"

When I heard that, I thought maybe that's what the flicker in Dad's eyes meant. Maybe it was his way of saying, "Ron, I did get it right. I did."

CHAPTER 13

PRAISE AND VICTORY

⌐

That first Sunday morning after the protest, after another sleepless night, and while new death threats and slurs were still being posted online, I got ready for church. That used to mean a morning spent in prayer, putting on my suit, and heading out the door with my Bible. Now my routine included a call to the security detail I'd hired to make sure they were en route and strapping on my loaded gun. I had to be ready for anything. As I smiled and greeted people at the door that morning, I could see the concern on their faces. Some looked at me as if they were surveying damage after a storm. In their eyes I saw the question, *How long will it take to rebuild?*

Mentally and physically, I was exhausted. In the past thirty-six hours, the enemy had hit me the hardest I'd ever been hit, and while I knew God was with me, I also felt He was watching to see how I would fight back. As a preacher, I'd been here before.

When we first moved to Houston, I had restarted my carpet-cleaning business that I ran from the back of a trailer and stored in a rented boat shed. One Sunday morning, I left church feeling great, proud of the way I'd preached on how Elisha fed his money-making oxen to the people and then set out after Elijah and a double portion of anointing. But when we got home, I learned that somebody had stolen all of my carpet-cleaning equipment. I called the police, and the first thing the officer said was, "Welcome to Houston." I knew then that my business was gone.

I went back to the church, knelt down, and prayed, "God, I need Your help." I was scared because the church wasn't big enough to support us, and I needed the money from my business to pay bills and buy groceries. I prayed louder, "God, I've *got* to have a miracle. I don't know what to do." But my prayers seemed to hit the ceiling and crumble. So I changed gears and started in on a complaining prayer that went something like, "God, I've done all of this for You. I moved my family here and trusted You, believed in You, and now this has happened."

When I was done squalling, the Lord spoke to my spirit and said, "You're going to make it, but you're also going to learn something along the way. You can either frown, pout, or be upset—and, if you do, I'm still going to bring you through it because you're My son, and I love you. Or, you can face this and go through it with a smile and not complain. And, after I bring you through, you will know My victory."

I went home to Stacey and told her, "We will not frown or cry about this, and we will not look back because God's going to make a way." And He did. Since that day, we have been in full-time ministry with no additional income.

But this time was different. Now, so much more had been stolen than just equipment. My name and my reputation as a pastor and a football coach had been taken from me and dragged through the mud. How much more can you destroy a man's character than to call him a slave master on television, not to mention the security threat to my family and my church. It was cruel and unfair, yet in my heart I knew that God expected me to react the same way — to follow Him through the darkness to victory.

As any believer knows, when you're hurting like that, the last thing you feel like doing is praising the Lord. Yet that's where His victory lives, between praise and worship. We started the Sunday service, and as Stacey led the singing, I felt the Lord strengthening me. I stood there on the platform and let the lyrics about His love and His majesty wash over me. *What a mighty God we serve. What a mighty God we serve.*

There is power in worship when Christians come together in one accord and praise God, especially when they sing the old hymns. I believe God gave to certain saints lyrics that were much more than songs. Some, like these, became anthems of the church:

> *Onward, Christian soldiers, marching as to war,*
> *With the cross of Jesus going on before!*
> *Christ, the royal Master, leads against the foe;*
> *Forward into battle, see His banners go!*
>
> *Amazing Grace, how sweet the sound*
> *That saved a wretch like me,*

I once was lost, but now am found,
Was blind but now I see.

On a hill far away, stood an old rugged cross,
The emblem of suffering and shame,
And I love that old cross where the dearest and best,
For a world of lost sinners was slain.

Blessed assurance, Jesus is mine;
O what a foretaste of glory divine!
Heir of salvation, purchase of God,
Born of His Spirit, washed in His blood.

Rock of Ages, cleft for me,
Let me hide myself in Thee;
Let the water and the blood,
From Thy wounded side which flowed,
Be of sin the double cure;
Save from wrath and make me pure.

Verses like these remind the church to stand up for Christ and from their hearts pledge allegiance to Him. I grew up on these songs in a time when the church was the church, and we weren't too proud to admit that we were sinners who needed a Savior. I realize that's looked down on today, but I'm still going to preach what the Word of God says and testify as to who Jesus Christ is to me: my Savior, my Lord, my Master, and my King. He is my life, and the one I live for. Christ is my everything.

After our time of praise and worship, I stepped up to the pulpit and prayed:

> Father, we thank You today. Thank You for Your mercy and Your grace. Lord, we thank You for all You've done in our lives, and all that You're going to do. I pray today that You will bless the hearts and lives of those here in service this morning as only You can do. Lord, only Your Holy Spirit can touch and pierce the hearts of men. God, we ask today that Your Holy Spirit would flow through this church. God we pray that Your Holy Spirit will move and touch those hearts. Lord, we pray for Your mighty hand to change those who are bound and twisted, those who are bound by alcohol and drug addiction, Lord, and those bound by hate and racism. Lord we pray that You will reach down and touch those today who are sick in their bodies. Lord, I just ask You today for strength for our congregation and for our families. Lord, we thank You this morning, and we just give You praise and glory for who You are. In Jesus's mighty, wonderful name. Amen.

In a church our size, it's noticeable when people stay home. Several of our folks weren't there that morning, and I didn't blame them. They were scared to come, I believe, after seeing the trash on social media and ugly words like "racist" and "white supremacist" attached to my name. Keeping steady church attendance is a struggle that every pastor knows. When Stacey and I started this church fourteen years ago, everyone we knew told us it was a bad idea. But God said do it, so we did.

Victory & Praise Worship Center started in a hotel conference room. When I called to rent it, the lady asked how many people we had in our congregation because the room only seated twenty-five. "No problem," I said, "we've only got five—me, my wife, and our three kids."

I got the word out best I could that we had started a church, and the next Sunday we had our first service. We played some music and worshipped the Lord in that large, empty room. Just as I was about to preach, a man came in and sat down. One man. The other nineteen chairs stayed empty.

Now, all these years later, I was seeing empty chairs again but for a completely different reason. It wasn't because our church was just getting started and no one knew about it. And it wasn't because of my messages; I only preach the Word of God. It was because people suddenly hated me for loving America, and hateful people, we've all learned, do dangerous things. These chairs were empty because people were afraid to come to church. It was the elephant in the room, and I had to address it:

> Don't be scared of the liberals. Don't be scared
> of those who hate America. Don't be scared of
> those who disagree with you because you have a
> different view. That's what America is all about.

It's a sad day when a pastor has to have a pistol to come to church. It's a bad day. A bad day. But I thank God still to be an American. I thank God still for my liberties. The thing is, the conservatives and those who believe as I do are so quiet. We're peaceful people. We don't try to get out and break stuff and burn stuff down and hurt people to get our way. We let people speak without trying to stop them from speaking, but that's not the way they are. On social media, I've been blasted, I mean blasted. To hear them tell it, I'm the biggest racist in the world, and I hate all black people. I guarantee you: that is not the truth. Racists don't come with the intention to start a multicultural church where everybody is welcome.

And I don't know of anybody—of any color—who has ever been to this church and not been welcomed. People who come to this church know that I hug them, I love them, and I care about them. I'll pray with them, I'll marry them, and I'll bury them just like I would anybody else because there is no difference. Each one is a soul, and I love them. I love all people because God created them all. I don't agree with injustice against anybody, but just because you take a stand doesn't mean that you agree with somebody being mistreated. I

don't agree with anyone who would mistreat
another person — especially a person of color.

That was a tough Sunday. What made it bearable was
seeing my football players there — players from every season
I'd coached — all wearing their Sharks jerseys. Most of them
didn't attend my church, but they came that morning with
their folks to support me — something I will always remember.

Seeing all those teal jerseys mixed in with the rest of the
congregation made me think about how God had brought
the two together — the church and the football program — into
one ministry. God remembered what I had given up some
twenty years earlier to go into full-time ministry, and He
rewarded that faithfulness, I believe, by giving me the opportunity to coach high school-level football. As a pastor, I made
sure that my ministry always took priority over the football
program, but I also wanted people to understand that the
football program was an important part of my ministry. To
me, they were never two different things.

People at church need to hear the Word of God and experience Christian fellowship. It's not always easy living this
life of faith, and there are times when we all need a hand up
the mountain. Boys who play football also need to hear the
Word of God, feel part of a team, and know that someone
cares about them and their futures. Both were part of the
ministry that God gave me and equipped me to carry out.

The boys I coached were fifteen to nineteen years old,
depending on when they graduated, and I learned quickly that
they're dealing with a lot more than I ever did at their ages.

Most of them were born after 9/11 to parents who remember what life was like before the Twin Towers fell. In one sense, you could say they were raised on defense in a new, reactive America that said, "If you can't beat 'em, don't offend 'em."

Today's liberal media is doing its best to sell boys on the idea that masculinity is toxic, and it's somehow wrong to be athletic or manly. Seeds planted twenty years ago by liberals into public school curriculums now have deep roots in the LGBTQ agenda, which has little boys and girls questioning their God-given genders and pushing legislation that requires them to use the same restrooms.

Today's teens grew up communicating on cell phones, with human emotions reduced to emojis and relationships dumbed down to "he said, she said" exchanges that can escalate from rudeness to sarcasm to hate in a social media second. No wonder so many boys are losing themselves to hours on end playing video games that are nothing like Pac-Man or Donkey Kong and everything like real-life killing.

Clearly, there's a need in this country to bring boys back to the basics, back to old-fashioned, face-to-face competition, and for decades, football has done that. It's good for a boy to grind a cleated toe into the ground, look an opponent square in the eye, and pray that he's prepared enough to endure a game where there will be winners and losers.

My coaching style is a blend of what I picked up from my football coaches and from my years in the Marine Corps. Over time, I developed a couple of drill sergeant-like phrases that the boys liked to hear.

On the field, I'd yell, "You're burning daylight, boys!" and they'd all laugh. Other times I'd holler, "All right, get on the line, boys!" Some of my former players have told me, "We always waited for you to say that one, Coach."

My first year of coaching, one thing I did was to make my own tire flipping drill. I had all these tires, different sizes, except for this one huge tractor tire, which I put at the end of the line. I'd make the boys flip and pull those smaller tires, and when they got down to that tractor tire, it was already in their minds that it would be the heaviest, but when they flipped it, they found out that it was the lightest tire out there. They'd laugh and yell, "There ain't nothing to this, Coach!"

Football is also a great example of teaching kids that when you're hurt or you're down, you push yourself. Don't give up, and don't quit. As a coach, I was teaching young men to push themselves beyond what they thought they could do. The average player, for example, goes out there, and he doesn't want to run twenty sprints, but you push him to run twenty. Once he runs those, he understands—I can run twenty. So then you ask him to run twenty-five. He does it, and he understands—I can run twenty-five.

So it's football practice, but it's also practice in showing boys how to face obstacles without fear and prepares them to tackle bigger things as they go along. Learning that at a young age can go a long way in life.

Sometimes, after practicing for a couple of hours in the hot Texas sun, I'd say, "Boys, some of you are hurting today, and you didn't feel like coming to practice, but you're here. You pushed yourself through practice, and that's a great example of what life's going to be like when you're married with kids. There will be days when you're sick, and you don't feel like going to work, but you have to go because your babies need to eat."

But football isn't all hard work. There is also camaraderie. From my own experience as a player, I know how easy it is to bond to a coach who is trying to help you in life. I tried to be that kind of coach. Many times I told the boys, "I'm always here for you. My door is always open, and I'm just a phone call away if you ever need me." Of course I'd lighten that up with, "If you call me from jail, I won't post your bail, but I will come and visit you." Or, I'd joke with them saying, "When you all get girlfriends . . . Aww, who am I kidding? Y'all are so ugly you won't never find one," and they'd crack up, laughing.

My players knew that I cared about them because when trouble hit, or they needed someone to talk to, they called. One of those calls came late at night, after one of my players and his brother were in a car wreck. Their mom offered to call their church pastor, but the boys told her no. "Call Coach and have him come pray for us." And I did.

I've had team parents call and ask me if I'd talk to their son. "We feel like you can get through to him," they'd say. Usually it was an issue with attitude. Boys that age tend to get a little feisty, especially with their moms; I don't know why, but I remember I did. "Your momma loves you," I'd remind them, "and you've got to be respectful of her. If you don't, you'll always regret it." I'd share with them how I'd shut out my own momma at that age and still regretted it. Sometimes that's all it takes—a good listen and some understanding.

Other times, it takes a lot more. We had one family in our football program that took in a kid whose mom was a drug addict and his dad had been murdered. After his first practice with us, he came back out to the field where I was and talked with me for a few minutes.

He said, "Coach, you'd never want to come to my house because it looks like where a crack addict lives."

"Really?" Inside, my heart ached for this boy who had been through so much.

"Yeah. You wouldn't want to come to my house."

When he said that, I thought, *I would have never even met you had it not been for this football program, let alone know how much you're hurting and need the Lord in your life.*

And that's the whole thing—a boy like that might never feel comfortable enough to come to a church and talk to a pastor, but he will talk to his coach on a football field. How many times I've experienced that, humbled each time a player of mine asked, "Coach, can I come talk to you?" To me, there was no greater compliment.

I thank God that He allowed me to serve Him as both a pastor and a coach because it brought more people to the saving knowledge of Christ, which is what I am called to do.

The most important part of any church service is the altar call, and that Sunday, when it felt like my world was crashing down around me, was no different. After preaching about the name of Jesus—the name under heaven given among men, whereby we must be saved—I asked everyone in the sanctuary to stand as I prayed:

Father, I thank You today for Your love and Your mercy. I thank You for Your grace, Father. I thank You today for changing lives and touching hearts. I thank You for all that You've done, Lord, in our lives, I thank You. Now Lord, I ask You this morning that You'd move across this room. Lord, that You would give strength and encouragement to each and every man, woman, and child here today. Let us understand and realize that until we accept Christ, there will be no peace in our lives.

Next comes the plea that the Lord allows His servants to make on His behalf. These are the times, as a pastor, that I've always felt closest to the Lord, as if He's standing right beside me, watching and waiting.

So many are troubled today. They don't know how to find peace. Just simply ask Jesus into your heart. He'll begin to change and touch you. This morning, I'm not going to embarrass you, I'm not going to try to bring you to the front. I'm just going to ask across this room, when I count to three, if you say in your heart, "Brother Ron, I want to accept Jesus as my personal Lord and Savior; I want to ask Him into my heart to wash me with His blood and to be my Savior," I'm going to count to three, and when I do, I simply want you to

look up at me — make eye contact with me —
then I'm going to know, and I'm going to lead
everybody in a prayer, and we're all going to
pray together.

One, do you believe that Jesus is the answer?
Two, do you trust Him and know that He's the
one you need?
Three, would you be honest before Him today . . .

Before I could finish that last sentence, eyes started
locking with mine, and when I saw whose they were, my
voice cracked as I started to pray. "Say this prayer with me
if you would: Lord Jesus, I love You today, and I want to ask
You into my heart to be my Lord and to be my Savior. I ask
You to wash away my sins and to write my name in Your
book of life as I place my faith in You and Your finished work
at Calvary. Amen."

Five boys wearing Sharks jerseys accepted Christ that
morning, and there it was — victory. Not mine, but the Lord's.

CHAPTER 14

MORE THAN JUST FOOTBALL

⌐

By summer of 2018, it was painfully clear that we weren't going to have enough boys signed up to field a football team for the coming season. On July 12, I posted on Facebook: *"With a sad heart I have to announce that the V&P Sharks will not field a football team in 2018. I want to thank God for all the great young men and families that have made the Sharks football program so special over the last six years."*

I went on to give reasons for my decision: too many graduating seniors leaving the team, several other six-man teams were folding, parental concerns over their sons getting concussions.

But that wasn't all of it. When I started my football program, I heard myself telling the boys over and over again that what they were doing at every practice, what they were learning—"It's more than just football." Eventually, that became our team's motto. And what it meant to me then was that coaching was more than pushing players to run harder and throw farther; it was also about teaching young men respect—for their families, their teammates, and themselves. Now, that saying has come to mean something different.

That night, as the national anthem played, and a player of mine decided to kneel, and another decided to a raise his fist in the air, I realized that contempt and hatred for our country is capable of wearing the same uniform as players who love and respect America. Like their NFL heroes, Larry and CJ used a patriotic moment and a football uniform to make it easier for the public to notice, in the row of their teammates, that one was down on a knee and another had raised a fist. And, like their mentors, they used a football game with a built-in audience to echo their message: "We don't believe in Old Glory. We want something new." And the new part has changed the national image of professional football in this country.

I'm sad that I missed coaching the 2018 season, but I thank God that I got to coach six-man football when I did. And I'm thankful for every single player that He sent my way, including Larry and CJ. I still care about those boys, and I hold no grudges. In fact, I gave CJ a clear letter of transfer so that he could play on another football team. I want him to keep playing because I understand all of the good that football can do for a boy. I remember what it did for me growing up, and I'm so thankful that I know what it is to play high school football on a Friday night in America, the way it used to be.

But now, after seeing how football has been manipulated these past two years by protesters, the Sharks team motto has come to mean more. When I think about our football program, and what all those games and seasons meant to the coaches and the parents and the players, I realize what a rare experience that is these days, that sense of community and family — it really was more than just football. When word got out that there would be no team for the 2018 season, the assistant coaches and parents got together to throw me a surprise "Thank You, Coach" party. They even got Stacey, Lynzie, and Kerstin involved to help throw me off the scent.

On July 29, when Stacey and I walked into Iguana Joe's restaurant, a large number of my former players along with many of their parents and the coaches with their families, stood up and applauded, and the sound, to me, was like a twenty-one-gun salute.

Each one of the players came up to me, looked me square in the eye, and shook my hand. Each one, in his own way, told me what being on my team meant to him. One of the best parts of the evening was hearing about the bright futures ahead, especially for these young men:

Ryan Hartzog would be the first Shark to play football at the college level. He'll be playing in Wisconsin this year as a quarterback. Greg Carman was headed to Texas A&M. Carlos Gomez would attend a college in Dallas. Yale Jay made the cross-country team for Dallas Baptist University. Samuel Branham and Caleb Sammon would be attending community colleges in Houston. And Robert Odom is currently serving in the US Navy.

It had always been my dream to coach my son Chase throughout his high school years. Now, I wouldn't have that opportunity. I did arrange for him to play for Tomball

Christian where he's a starter as a receiver, cornerback, and kicker.

I realized that while the football program may not ever field another team, the V&P Sharks would live on through the young men who had played in my program, and that was a very good feeling.

The parents at the party were beaming, full of pride, as they should be. I know how proud I am of Chase, and I tell him every chance I get. I believe that's the one thing every boy seeks in life — approval from his dad. I grew up without that, and even though I learned to find comfort in my heavenly Father's love for me, I was always a little jealous of boys who had the kind of dads who always stood behind them, no matter what, and said to them those simple words, "Son, I love you, and I'm proud of you."

When my family and I got home from the party, I had no idea that what I had wanted to hear my whole life but never did would come from my own son. Chase hugged me, and with tears in his eyes said, "I love you, Dad. I'm really proud of you, and I want you to know that I've always got your back." Tears ran down my face. I said, "Thank you, son. I love you, too."

The words I needed to hear never came from my father, or from any other man who had influence on my life. They came from the man I had raised — my son, Chase — and it was the greatest gift that he could have ever given to me.

Later that night, after everyone else had gone to bed, I sat in the living room, thinking. It was starting to sink in that my football program was over. That part of my ministry was over. What now?

Of course, the devil was right there to whisper, "You're not a coach anymore. You lost your program, just like I said you would."

But almost as quick God brought to my mind a memory that always encourages me. It was a time when our car stalled on the highway late one night. Stacey and baby Lynzie were with me, and I managed to pull the car to the side of the curve in the road—an awkward place—but that's as far as I could get it before the car gave out. Parked on the outside curve of that road in the dark, I didn't think anyone would see us, let alone stop and offer help. We sat there for a few minutes and watched car after car whiz by.

I got out and opened the hood to see if I could do anything to get us going again. When the car had stalled earlier that week, I had prayed, and the engine started up. So I prayed again, "God, I need help." And then, as if God didn't already know, I added, "We're broke down out here on this country road." As I was shutting the hood, I heard the Lord speak to my heart. He said, "I've got others."

That was not the answer I needed to hear. "You've got others? What does that mean? I need somebody to help *now*." Just then a man driving a big semi rolled up and pulled off the road right in front of us. I walked up to the cab, and he waved for me to get in. I hollered over his engine, "Can I get my wife and baby?" The truck driver smiled and nodded. I held onto Lynzie while Stacey climbed up into the cab. Halfway up, she turned and smiled at me real big. I handed the baby to her, and when I got into the cab, I saw why she had smiled. Gospel music was playing on the radio and there on the dash was a big, worn Bible. Suddenly, what God had said to me made sense: "I've got others."

From then on, I knew that whenever I was in need, if I would just trust God, He had others, like that truck driver, who loved Him and could be used by Him to help the people of God. In my heart, I also knew that God could turn what appeared to be a defeat in my life into His victory. That's when He gave me the idea to start holding special evangelistic-style "Stand Up America" meetings at churches around the country. I share with Christians a condensed version of the story you're reading now as an example of the hate unleashed against anyone who stands for Christ or this country. As believers, we need to understand that when Jesus said, *"You shall be hated of all men for My name's sake,"* He meant it. In America, Christians don't suffer anywhere near the persecution as our brothers and sisters serving the Lord in other countries, where the cost for confessing Christ as Lord is your life.

I've found that there are still Christians in this country who know and understand how blessed they are to live in America, and they are willing to take a public stand against sin and for biblical morality even if it means facing lawsuits, ridicule, or slander. Almost daily now we read in the news about some Christian worker, teacher, or coach who is threatened with the loss of his job—and most certainly his reputation—just because he refused to support same-sex marriage, failed to use the right pronoun when referring to a transgender student, or prayed with his football team on public school property. I thank God for these Christians who are standing up and fighting, hard, for their religious freedoms in this country. God, give us more of them.

At the same time, we're seeing cities around the country cower to the threat of lawsuits that say things like, "Remove your statue of the Ten Commandments from the public property of city hall. We don't care that it was donated by the people and has been a fixture in the community for more than seventy-five years. Move it, or else." Replicas of crosses in public parks and on college campuses, now suddenly offensive, are also coming down at an alarming rate.

Satan is behind all of this. He hates America for two reasons: her export of the gospel around the world and her support of Israel. As an ally to Israel, God will continue to bless America, and the devil knows that. That's why he's fighting so hard to curse this country because without America, Satan knows that the gospel will stop going into other countries like it does now. He also knows that if Christians refuse to stand up for Christ and the gospel, they will lose their religious liberties in America to a world — his world — that rejects all truth of God's Word.

I love my country. I love America. So far, I've lived fifty-two of her two hundred and forty-two years, and during that time, I've learned this: the love that a person has for his country can be measured by the respect he shows for his country. So, when I see America's historical statues pulled down, our national monuments defaced, the Pledge of Allegiance silenced in public schools, and "The Star-Spangled Banner" disrespected, I can only conclude that the people who do these things do not love America. If they do love this country, then why are they trying so hard to deconstruct its DNA, erase its history, and split, if they could, the American atom?

I remember the first time I realized that not everybody loves this country. It was when the Vietnam War was beginning to end. I was just a kid, maybe seven years old, so I didn't understand all of the protesting and pain of it. Back then, all I knew about war was what I'd seen in movies: America won, the troops came home, and people celebrated.

So, on Jan. 23, 1973, when President Nixon announced on TV that an accord had been reached to end the Vietnam War—an accord that would "end the war and bring peace with honor,"[1] I expected some kind of patriotic response. Our local radio station announced that at 7:00 p.m. the next night, everybody was to honk their car horns in celebration of the war's end and to show respect for the veterans.

That next night, I remember watching the clock, waiting for 7:00 p.m. At 6:45, I couldn't wait another minute and went outside to stand in the driveway, next to our Gran Torino. Once the horns started, I wanted to be ready to honk ours. But 7:00 p.m. came and went, and not one neighbor honked a car horn. I didn't even see any neighbors come outside. I figured maybe I had gotten the time wrong and went back inside, but that wasn't it. No one honked for America or for the veterans, period.

So yes, there have always been Americans who don't love America the way I do, and that's disappointing because the United States is such a great country. Some people don't appreciate it because it's all they've experienced, but outside of these borders are people in poverty who long for just a taste of the many freedoms that we have.

I remember a trip I took to Madera, Mexico, to share the gospel with the people there. This was a very poor area, and part of our ministry was to distribute care packages, which included a few items of clothing, some toiletries, and small bags of beans and rice to the adults after they heard the gospel. One time, when I had finished preaching, this little boy, maybe five or six years old, came up behind me, tugging on my shirttail. He was talking away at me, but I didn't speak Spanish and couldn't understand him. I got one of the interpreters to translate what the boy was saying. "He says, 'Can I pleeeese help my mama and sisters? They couldn't come. My mama couldn't come.'"

I handed the boy one of the bundles, and the look on his face was like I'd given him a gold nugget. He smiled from ear to ear and then took off running down that dirt road. And you couldn't help but cry. Everybody there—we all started crying because he was so proud just to take that little bit of stuff home to his momma and sisters.

I'll never forget the gratitude in that little face. America is a compassionate nation, a giving nation. And what we give best to the world is the gospel of Jesus Christ. As much as that little bag of supplies may have helped that boy and his family, I believe the gospel message that he heard that day helped him more.

America was founded on Christian principles, which boil down to one word: freedom. We are free in this country to worship and preach however we want. The devil hates that. Most people, even a lot of Christians may not realize it, but all this division that we're seeing nowadays is really a spiritual battle, and to win, Christians need to band together.

As a pastor for more than twenty-five years, I know very well that Christians differ on some doctrine. But the one thing that has always united us is the cross of Christ. Faith in the redeeming shed blood of Jesus Christ — represented by His cross — is where salvation starts for every believer, so that's what every Christian has in common.

In a similar way, the one thread of unity for all Americans is the flag. It speaks for us as a nation, flying high and bright from US military installations; lowered to half-staff under the heavy weight of national mourning, and folded into a tight triangle of gratitude for a life of service and a death of honor.

I know, and most Americans know and understand, that if we lose that one common thread — that love and respect for country — then it won't be long before the freedoms we have unravel. So, how do we ensure that our love of country and respect continue? I found the answer to that question in coaching.

When the news media swarmed in to cover two teen protesters on my team, they never once talked to any of the other eleven players who are patriotic and who stood tall while the national anthem played. Had they been interviewed, those reporters could have told the world about some outstanding young men — young men who are part of the promise that God gave to me that day on the road when He said, "I have others." There are plenty of others out there who love America the way I do, and they will defend it.

I've had several people ask me if enduring all of the hate and the threats and having my reputation so severely damaged was worth it, just so I could look myself in the mirror and know that I did the right thing. My answer to that question is this: I never fought for my country on the battlefield, but I did fight for it on a football field by standing up for America's symbols — the national anthem and the flag. So, yes, it was more than worth it.

Outside of our church is a US flag that flies from a pole that I placed in the ground myself. I can see it from anywhere on the place — from the football field, the house, or the church — and it's always been a comfort to me, just knowing that it's there. When all of this happened, I found myself paying more attention to it, considering everything that those Stars and Stripes represent.

I learned that when our Founding Fathers were adopting a flag, they did not assign official meaning to its colors, as some people think. At least one expert believes they adopted the same colors used in the Union Jack of England. It was for the colors used in the Great Seal that they declared the white to mean purity and innocence, the red stripes, hardiness and valor; and the blue field, vigilance, perseverance, and justice.[2]

When it came to the flag, perhaps the Founding Fathers weren't as concerned with its colors as they were with what the flag itself represented to them: freedom at any cost.

I believe there's a lesson here. When it comes to the preservation of freedom in America, it's not the colors of our emblem that matter as much as the cost they represent. The red costs. The white costs. The blue costs.

That's why, when the national anthem plays, I stand, put my hand over my heart, and pray to God that the next generation will do the same. Because it's up to every generation in this country to answer the question raised in the last line of America's song: *"O say, does that star-spangled banner yet wave o'er the land of the free and the home of the brave?"*

ACKNOWLEDGMENTS

T rue to His word to me, God does have others — many others — and He's placed several of them across my path at just the right moment, not only to help but also to support and encourage me. And while I am grateful for every single one, I would be remiss not to acknowledge the Lord first for this book, which is only one page in my life, for He is the author and finisher of my faith.

I'm thankful that through the ministry of my football program, the V&P Sharks, the Lord was able to touch more hearts and lives thanks in great part to the tireless efforts of Jeff and Latonya Stracner, Greg Sammon, Eli Melton, Kris and Kathi Haller, Ron Fuller, Glen Fulcher, Mike Cheatham, Brian Branham, Steve and Jill Hadley, Gary and Paula Jones, Michael and Erin Roy, Dugan and Lanette Hartzog, Kristine Gerlich, Justin Klump, and especially Brad and Kenda Wilson. This team of faithful volunteers transformed a group of coaches, players, and parents into a family, and as far as I'm concerned, we will always be a Sharks family.

My love for football and desire to play the game with heart and class was inspired by the Christian example of Coach Glen Ward, and I wish every young man at least one Coach Ward in his life.

I also want to say something about my momma on this page. She always believed in me, always encouraged me, and always loved me, even when I lost my way in life. I know she will read this and say, "That's just what mommas do." But you and I know that not all mommas are like mine. I didn't always appreciate that as a teenage boy, but I cherish it now. Thank you, Momma.

When my sister Rhonda read an early copy of this book, she said something that siblings don't often tell each other: "I'm proud of you." (She also said she was glad that I didn't include any more of our childhood stories.) Rhonda, I know that you, too, didn't hear any encouragement from Dad growing up, but if a brother's words will do, know that I'm very proud of you and all that you've accomplished in your career and with your family.

When Stacey married me, she married into a life of ministry and football. Both are more than demanding, but she endured, with a smile, the long nights of driving to and from football games, and the twenty-plus hours a week that I spent coaching when I could have been helping more with her endless list of chores that make our lives at home and church run smooth. Our three amazing kids—Kerstin, Lynzie, and Chase—share Stacey's understanding and support for me, which means everything to a husband and father.

When the idea was first presented to me about writing this book, I didn't know where to start. That's when God sent one more semi-truck, this one driven by my good friend Stan Oliver, who made the production of this book possible. Along the way, we picked up the writing talents of Desiree Jones, who knew by heart the rest of the way home.

To all of you, God bless, and I love you.

NOTES

Preface

[1] Thomas M. Hammond, "William H. Carney: The First Black Soldier to Earn the Medal of Honor," *Military Times* online, February 5, 2018, https://www.militarytimes.com/military-honor/black-military-history/2018/02/06/william-h-carney-the-first-black-soldier-to-earn-the-medal-of-honor/.

[2] Jason Samenow, "Harvey dumped 33 trillion gallons on Texas, southern US," The Washington Post/The Mercury News, January 25, 2018, https://www.mercurynews.com/2018/01/25/harvey-dumped-33-trillion-gallons-on-texas-southern-us/.

[3] Savannah Labbe, "For Duty, Honor, and Family: Color Bearers in the Civil War," *The Gettysburg Compiler: On the Front Lines of History* online, January 25, 2017, https://gettysburgcompiler.org/2017/01/25/for-duty-honor-and-family-color-bearers-in-the-civil-war/.

[4] *The United States Service Magazine*, Vol. 1, No. 1, New York, 1864, 282.

Chapter 1

[1] Kimberly Amadeo, "Hurricane Harvey Facts, Damage and Costs," *The Balance* online, updated January 20, 2019, https://www.thebalance.com/hurricane-harvey-facts-damage-costs-4150087.

[2] Ibid.

[3] Ibid.

[4] Ibid.

[5] Jason Samenow, "Harvey dumped 33 trillion gallons on Texas, southern US," The Washington Post/The Mercury News, January 25, 2018, https://www.mercurynews.com/2018/01/25/harvey-dumped-33-trillion-gallons-on-texas-southern-us/.

[6] Ibid.

Chapter 3

[1] Mark Sandritter, "A Timeline of Colin Kaepernick's National Anthem Protest and the Athletes Who Joined Him," SBNation online, updated September 25, 2017, https://www.sbnation.com/2016/9/11/12869726/colin-kaepernick-national-anthem-protest-seahawks-brandon-marshall-nfl.

[2] Jennifer Chan, "Colin Kaepernick Did Not Stand During the National Anthem [Picture]," *SBNation* online, August 27, 2016, https://www.ninersnation.com/2016/8/27/12669048/colin-kaepernick-did-not-stand-during-the-national-anthem.

[3] Mike Florio, "Kaepernick Sits During National Anthem," *ProFootballTalk* on NBCSports.com, August 27, 2016, https://profootballtalk.nbcsports.com/2016/08/27/kaepernick-sits-during-national-anthem/.

[4] Chris Biderman, "Transcript: Colin Kaepernick Addresses Sitting During National Anthem," *NinersWire* online, August 28, 2016, https://ninerswire.usatoday.com/2016/08/28/transcript-colin-kaepernick-addresses-sitting-during-national-anthem/.

[5] Ibid.

[6] David Whitley, "Colin Kaepernick Making a Misguided Stand," *Orlando Sentinel* online," August 28, 2016, https://www.orlandosentinel.com/sports/nfl/os-colin-kaepernick-national-anthem-david-whitley-0829-20160828-column.html.

[7] Mike Florio, "Kaepernick Sits During National Anthem," *ProFootballTalk* on NBCSports.com, August 27, 2016, https://profootballtalk.nbcsports.com/2016/08/27/kaepernick-sits-during-national-anthem/.

[8] Armando Salguero, "Unrepentant Hypocrite Colin Kaepernick Defends Fidel Castro," *Miami Herald* online, November 25, 2016, https://www.

miamiherald.com/sports/spt-columns-blogs/armando-salguero/article117033883.html.

[9]Anthony DePalma, "Fidel Castro, Cuban Revolutionary Who Defied U.S., Dies at 90," *The New York Times* online, November 26, 2016, https://www.nytimes.com/2016/11/26/world/americas/fidel-castro-dies.html.

[10]Chuck Schilken, "Colin Kaepernick Says the Pigs on His Socks Were Only Meant to Represent 'Rogue Cops,'" *The Los Angeles Times* online, September 1, 2016, http://www.latimes.com/sports/nfl/la-sp-colin-kaepernick-socks-20160901-snap-htmlstory.html.

[11] Ibid.

[12]Matt Malocco, "NFL: Standing for National Anthem 'Not Required,'" NBC Sports.com, August 27, 2016, https://www.nbcsports.com/bayarea/49ers/nfl-standing-national-anthem-not-required.

[13]Sheil Kapadia, "Jeremy Lane Sits During National Anthem Ahead of Seahawks-Raiders," ESPN online, September 6, 2016, http://www.espn.com/nfl/story/_/id/17445208/jeremy-lane-seattle-seahawks-sits-national-anthem-oakland-raiders-game.

[14]Mark Sandritter, "A Timeline of Colin Kaepernick's National Anthem Protest and the Athletes Who Joined Him," *SBNation* online, updated September 25, 2017, https://www.sbnation.com/2016/9/11/12869726/colin-kaepernick-national-anthem-protest-seahawks-brandon-marshall-nfl.

[15]"Goodell Recognizes Kap's Right to Protest, Disagrees with Action," NFL.com Wire Reports, updated September 7, 2017, http://www.nfl.com/news/story/0ap3000000696136/article/goodell-recognizes-kaps-right-to-protest-disagrees-with-action.

[16]Jerry Tapp, "NFL Census: Data on Players' Race, Weight & Height," Heavy.com, updated September 24, 2014, https://heavy.com/sports/2014/09/what-percentage-of-nfl-players-are-black-white/.

[17]Nathan McDermott, "Trump on Kaepernick: 'Maybe He Should Find A Country That Works Better For Him,'" Buzzfeed News online, August 29, 2016, https://www.buzzfeednews.com/article/natemcdermott/trump-on-49ers-kaepernick-maybe-he-should-find-a-country-tha#.spEOGJxvv.

[18]Polina Marinova, "Colin Kaepernick Did Not Vote for Hillary Clinton or Donald Trump," Fortune.com, November 9, 2016, http://fortune.com

/2016/11/08/election-colin-kaepernick-donald-trump-hillary-clinton/.

[19]Douglas Ernst, "Steve Largent, Seahawks Legend: National Anthem Not the Time for 'Pot Shot' Activism, *The Washington Times* online, September 9, 2016, https://www.washingtontimes.com/news/2016/sep/9/steve-largent-seahawks-legend-national-anthem-not-/

[20]Bryan Armen Graham, "Mike Ditka to Colin Kaepernick: 'Get the Hell Out' If You Don't Like America," *The Guardian* online, September 23, 2016, https://www.theguardian.com/sport/2016/sep/23/mike-ditka-colin-kaepernick-get-the-hell-out-anthem-protest.

[21]Edward Helmore, "Super Bowl Sunday: Kick Back, Crack Open a Beer and Wait for the Anti-Trump Protests to Begin," *The Guardian* online, February 4, 2017, https://www.theguardian.com/sport/2017/feb/05/super-bowl-trump-protest-patriots-falcons-gaga.

[22]L. Lemons, "Black Lives Matter Protest outside Super Bowl 51," CW39 Houston online, updated February 5, 2017, https://cw39.com/2017/02/05/black-lives-matter-protest-at-super-bowl-51/.

[23]Martin Luther King, Jr., "Remaining Awake Through a Great Revolution," March 31, 1968, https://kinginstitute.stanford.edu/king-papers/documents/remaining-awake-through-great-revolution.

[24]Frank Pallotta, "More Than 111 Million People Watched Super Bowl LI," CNN Business online, February 7, 2017, https://money.cnn.com/2017/02/06/media/super-bowl-ratings-patriots-falcons/.

[25]Ahiza Garcia, "Super Bowl Ticket Prices Spike After Early Slump," CNNMoney/Sport online, February 13, 2017, https://money.cnn.com/2017/02/03/news/super-bowl-ticket-prices/index.html.

[26]Joe Martin, "Results Are In: How Much the 2017 Super Bowl Brought to Houston," *Houston Business Journal* online, May 25, 2017, https://www.bizjournals.com/houston/news/2017/05/25/results-are-in-how-much-the-2017-super-bowl.html

[27]Marcio Jose Sanchez, "Many Young Athletes Joining Colin Kaepernick's National Anthem Protest," CBS News online, September 14, 2016, https://www.cbsnews.com/news/many-young-athletes-joining-colin-kaepernicks-national-anthem-protest/.

[28]CBS News online/The Associated Press, "Football Coach Fired for Postgame Prayer Takes Action Against School," August 9, 2016, https://www.cbsnews.com/news/

washington-football-coach-fired-for-post-game-prayer-takes-action-against-school/.

Chapter 4

[1]Bryan Armen Graham, "Donald Trump Blasts NFL Anthem Protesters: 'Get That Son of a Bitch Off the Field,'" *The Guardian* online, September 23, 2017, https://www.theguardian.com/sport/2017/sep/22/donald-trump-nfl-national-anthem-protests.

[2] Ibid.

[3]Jon Herskovitz, "Two Houston-area High School Football Players Kicked Off Team for Protest," Reuters online, September 30, 2017, https://www.reuters.com/article/us-usa-trump-sports-texas/two-houston-area-high-school-football-players-kicked-off-team-for-protest-idUSKCN1C60V0.

[4]Adam Coleman, "Local High School Football Players Kicked Off Team After Protest During Anthem," *The Houston Chronicle* online, updated September 30, 2017, https://www.chron.com/sports/highschool/article/High-school-football-kicked-off-team-anthem-kneel-12242713.php.

[5] Ibid.

[6] Ibid.

[7]Todd Starnes, "Teen Football Players Kicked Off Team After Protesting National Anthem," Todd Starnes online, October 1, 2017, https://www.toddstarnes.com/uncategorized/teen-football-players-kicked-off-team-after-protesting-national-anthem/.

[8] Ibid.

[9] Barbara Goldberg, Dan Trotta, Peter Szekely, and Alex Dobuzinskis, "One Year Later, Las Vegas Honors 58 Killed in Mass Shooting," Reuters online, October 1, 2018, https://www.reuters.com/article/us-lasvegas-shooting/one-year-later-las-vegas-honors-58-killed-in-mass-shooting-idUSKCN1MB3CO.

[10]Jerome Solomon, "King Solomon's Mind: Coach Oversteps His Bounds with Protest Banishment," *Houston Chronicle* online, updated October 3, 2017, https://www.chron.com/sports/texas-sports-nation/article/King-Solomon-Mind-Coach-oversteps-bounds-protest-12243064.php.

[11] Ibid.

Chapter 5

[1] David Shedden, "Early TV Anchors," Poynter online, April 4, 2006, https://www.poynter.org/news/early-tv-anchors.

[2] The American Presidency Project, "Radio and Television Remarks Upon Signing the Civil Rights Bill," July 2, 1964, https://www.presidency.ucsb.edu/documents/radio-and-television-remarks-upon-signing-the-civil-rights-bill.

[3] BlackPast.org Online Reference Guide to African American History, "The Harlem 'Race Riot' of 1964," https://blackpast.org/aah/harlem-race-riot-1964.

[4] James Queally, "Watts Riots: Traffic Stop Was the Spark That Ignited Days of Destruction in L.A., *The Los Angeles Times* online, July 29, 2015, https://www.latimes.com/local/lanow/la-me-ln-watts-riots-explainer-20150715-htmlstory.html.

[5] *Freedomways Quarterly Review of the Negro Freedom Movement,* Volume 7, Issue 2, Spring Second Quarter 1967. Cover quote for editorial, "The Measure of a Man." http://voices.revealdigital.com/cgi-bin/independentvoices?a=d&d=IBJBJF19670002.1.1.

[6] Larry Wines, "The Story of the 1975–1976 American Freedom Train," FreedomTrain.org, http://www.freedomtrain.org/american-freedom-train-home.htm.

Chapter 8

[1] Brittany Taylor, "Crosby Coach Kicks 2 High School Football Players Off Team After Anthem Protest," September 30, 2017, https://www.click2houston.com/news/crosby-coach-kicks-2-high-school-football-players-off-team-after-anthem-protest.

[2] ABC 13 Eyewitness News (KTRK), Foti Kallergis, "2 Football Players Kicked Off Private School Team After Taking Knee During National Anthem," October 1, 2017, https://abc13.com/sports/football-players-kicked-off-team-for-taking-a-knee/2473284/.

[3] Ibid.

[4] *Frances & Friends,* SonLife Broadcasting Network, transcript, October 3, 2017.

Chapter 10

[1]National Museum of the Marine Corps, "Lore of the Core: The Eagle, Globe and Anchor," https://www.usmcmuseum.com/lore-of-the-corps.html.

[2] Collin Hoeferlin, "Anniversary of Beirut Marine Barracks Bombing," MarineParents.com, October 22, 2013, https://marineparents.com/marinecorps/beirut-bombing.asp

[3] Kelly O'Sullivan, USMC Marine Corps Air Ground Combat Center Twentynine Palms, California, 60th Anniversary Commemoration, 1952–2012, https://www.29palms.marines.mil/Portals/56/Docs/G5/Publications/SpecialPub.MCAGCC60thAnniversary.pdf?ver=2013–09–16–185548–900.

Chapter 11

[1]Facebook, Victory & Praise Worship Center/Reviews. https://www.facebook.com/pg/vandpwc/reviews/?ref=page_internal.

[2] John Tedesco, Vincent Davis, Jasper Scherer, and Guillermo Contreras, "A Day of Death and Heroism in Sutherland Springs," San Antonio Express-News, November 12, 2017, https://www.expressnews.com/news/local/article/A-day-of-death-and-heroism-in-Sutherland-Springs-12348306.php.

Chapter 14

[1]President Richard Nixon's 14 Addresses to the Nation on Vietnam, "Achieving 'Peace with Honor' — 1969 to 1973," Richard Nixon Foundation/Library/Museum, https://www.nixonfoundation.org/2017/09/president-richard-nixons-14-addresses-nation-vietnam/.

[2]Nicole Greenstein, "Why the U.S. Flag is Red, White and Blue," *Time* online, July 4, 2013, http://swampland.time.com/2013/07/04/why-the-u-s-flag-is-red-white-and-blue/.

ABOUT THE AUTHOR

R onnie Mitchem is an ordained minister with more than twenty-five years of ministry experience. As a pastor, he has led five different churches in Alabama, Florida, Mississippi, and Texas, including Victory & Praise Worship Center, which he founded in 2004. As an evangelist, Mitchem has preached across the continental United States and abroad. Mitchem's life experiences as a former US Marine and businessman enrich his calling and preaching style, which God has anointed to reach thousands for the cause of Christ in churches, on the street, and inside prisons. Mitchem resides in Crosby, Texas, with his wife, Stacey. They have three children: Kerstin, Lynzie, and Chase. This is his first book.

CPSIA information can be obtained
at www.ICGtesting.com
Printed in the USA
LVHW020901170619
621442LV00002B/393